Advanced Magick
for Beginners

by

Alan Chapman

First published 2008
by Aeon Books Ltd.
London W5
www.aeonbooks.co.uk

British Library Cataloguing in Publication Data
A C.I.P. is available for this book from the British Library.

ISBN-13: 978-1-90465-841-2

Om Gam.
I bow to Ganapati.

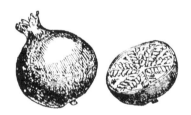

Contents

Acknowledgments

This book is dedicated to my lazy chela, Duncan Barford.

I would like to thank OR for the vision, Lord Ganesha for opening the way, Tezcatlipoca for taking an interest, AC for the teachings, RAW for the handover, the BIS for the most fun I've had in my life, and the One True Body of Saints for all their love and support.

INTRODUCTION

OR:

'THE PURPOSE OF THIS BOOK'

Investigating the Western tradition of magick can be confusing at the best of times, let alone for a person who is at the beginning of their magical journey. There is the near-impenetrable transcendentalism of early twentieth-century magical texts, the moralistic environmentalism of the modern Pagan movement, the popular naive sentimentality of the New Age and the almost cartoon-like practical materialism of some postmodern authors. Where are we supposed to look for a basic introduction to magick, when there doesn't appear to be a consensus on what magick is, let alone a reason for why we might want to practice it?

However this confusion around the fundamental nature of magick is in itself a fairly recent development. Historically, magick has a very specific purpose as a two-thousand-year-old sacred tradition peculiar to the West. Beginning in Hellenistic Greece, where it was taught by the likes of Plato and Plotinus, it was absorbed into Christianity by pseudo-Dionysius, then forced underground to become alchemy during the Dark Ages. It resurfaced through John Dee and Rosicrucianism in the sixteenth century, and later manifested as the European occult revival of the nineteenth and twentieth centuries. Over the years it has survived near extinction through religious persecution and deliberate misrepresentation. Today it has to contend with the rot of extreme postmodernism, which is the principal cause of the tradition's current obfuscation.

Postmodern thought is often misunderstood, and the concept of pluralism—the recognition of many contexts and the understanding that no one context is privileged in and of itself—is often confused with the absurd notion that every approach, culture and tradition is commensurate and of equal merit. In terms of magick, the purpose and teachings of our magical heritage in the West has been replaced with this extreme ethical standpoint, and some magicians even claim that the Western Tradition is actually a syncretic mish-mash of any and all of the magical religions practiced in the West. Is it any wonder we can't find a basic consensus on what magick is?

Thankfully, as inconvenient as extreme postmodernism may be, the truth of the matter doesn't require a democracy, nor is the Western Tradition simply a body of work that requires recovery. On the contrary: direct, personal experience of its core practice can teach us everything we need to know.

Therefore the fresh perspective on magick presented here is the result of over a decade's personal research, experiment and revelation. The fundamental purpose and practice of magick is the same as it ever was, and so although this work appears to offer a new paradigm it should be noted that this is nothing more than a timely rejuvenation of the surface features of the Tradition, something which has already occurred periodically throughout magick's long and troubled history.

CHAOS MAGIC

The publication of Peter Carroll's *Liber Null* in 1978 ushered in the last revolution in the surface features of magick, spawning a movement that eventually became known as 'Chaos Magic[1]'. With its emphasis on practicality and on looking at what actually 'works', *Liber Null* was different to previous magical texts, in that for the first time a commonality of technique behind magical effects was revealed.

However a subtle shift in focus came about as a result of this experiment in reductionism. Magick became the technology of using belief as a tool, and any given world view could be commandeered to provide personal satisfaction for the postmodern magician.

The influence of Chaos Magic has been pervasive, and present day occultism is essentially comprised of a handful of techniques endlessly recycled and translated by fame hungry 'occult

---

1. For more on Chaos Magic see *Liber Null and Psychonaut* and *Liber Kaos* by Peter Carroll; *Condensed Chaos* by Phil Hine; and *Chaotopia!* by Dave Lee.

stars', who actually believe they are offering transformation for the masses. It is a testament to Carroll that these techniques can be found in the first five pages of *Liber Null*. It is also telling of where reductionism has led magick when we see that the rest of *Liber Null* (which covers topics such as 'The Great Work', morality, reincarnation and permanent 'magical consciousness') is no longer considered magick at all.

Now, thirty years on, Chaos Magic (like much of magical culture) has fallen prey to extreme postmodernism. The Tradition has degenerated to such an extent that many of its practitioners now claim it is just a theory, despite the fact that it is clearly synonymous with a body of work and an unquestionable aesthetic. Instead of attempting to understand magick by *discovering* what the practice has to offer *through experience*, these extreme postmodern magicians deconstruct our rich and varied magical heritage *to one correct answer* ('all truth is relative'—except for their omniscient knowledge that this is so) with the benefits of magical practice reduced to immediate material effect: 'I *already* know everything magick has to offer—and anything else that isn't a material result isn't magick'.

Before Chaos Magic came along the Western Tradition was in danger of being lost behind a wall of overly complex symbolism and antiquated morality, more or less existing as the pastime of ridiculous armchair eccentrics. Chaos Magic breathed new life into it, making it a practice once again, and this time in a manner accessible to all. The contribution of postmodern thought to Western magical culture should therefore be celebrated. Nevertheless, it is time to address the detriment of extreme postmodernism. I hope this book will do this through providing a new, revitalised expression of our magical heritage.

THE NEXT BIG THING

Today, 'occult' no longer means 'hidden'. The torture and murder of magicians is now quite low on the government's list of things to do. Although magick is still not accepted as a bone fide spiritual discipline by the media at large, the number of people investigating it as a valid world view is evident from the steady growth of popular interest in dumbed-down versions of magical traditions, such as Rav Berg's Kabbalah, or the proliferation of published works by the 'next generation' of young magicians, where scholarship is considered inappropriate, sentimentalism rife and reasoning power painfully absent. Yet this is not to be mourned; for the occult as a commodity—just like the popularisation of alien abductions, the return of Buddha and increasingly complex crop circles— is indicative of a growing trend towards a proliferation of magical thought in the public sphere, and a re-orientation of Western culture towards the esoteric.

At present, magick may incur ridicule—this is clearly demonstrated through the embarrassment felt by the current occult scene towards the term itself. However this very embarrassment indicates an increasing openness towards magical practice—

something that has never occurred before on such a scale. Some feel that calling it 'a technology' saves their blushes, but this is an unnecessary exercise in finding public acceptance. Increasingly, the word 'magick' is being used more and more in its original sense. Ask yourself—do you think that our forebears who were burnt at the stake would have been embarrassed to call themselves 'magicians'?

SIGNING ON

Magick is now an opportunity for more people than ever before.

This book is a sign-post.

1. Nothing Up My Sleeve

Or:

'What To Expect From Magick'

Below are the two most frequently asked questions about magick, with my answers.

Q: What is magick?

A: There isn't a man, woman or child on this planet that does not know what magick is. Don't ask silly questions.

Q: Does magick work?

A: No.

Still Reading?

The only way you will ever answer either of these questions, to any degree of satisfaction, is to actually *do some magick*.

I can tell you what to expect: sometime after you have performed a magical act, whether to bring about a specific event, divine the future or communicate with a spirit, the result will manifest via the means available, and *you will get exactly what you ask for*.

But then, I can tell a virgin what to expect from sex, however that expectation is incapable of conveying a modicum of the experience, and can in no way account for the effect of that experience upon the self. It should also be noted that, just as in sex, no one is good the first time they do magick, and it takes a degree of practice before you can even begin to do it properly.

Remember: failure means you need more practice. If the first time you hear music is at your first piano lesson, would it not be a great folly to dismiss the idea that you might one day be a concert pianist, or to refuse to even consider the existence of Beethoven's Fifth Symphony, based on the results of that lesson?

So what are the implications of the magical experience upon the self? Beyond performing the odd ritual here and there, what can a novice expect from a future as a practicing magician?

GETTING WHAT YOU WANT

Being a magician means you get to make wishes that come true.

What you can experience through magick is limited only by your imagination.

How you experience a magical result is limited only by the available means of manifestation.

Yes, you can use magick to obtain money, sex and power; as such, these things will occur along the lines of any other 'real' event, in the form of a synchronicity. For instance, if you do some magick to win some money, the next day you might visit a betting shop, put some money on a horse and win. But if you do some magick to 'fly like Superman', you will no doubt experience the result via a dream, because that is the available means by which the result can manifest. Unless of course you accidentally fall out of the 53rd floor window at the office fancy dress party.

In the same sense, you can use magick to raise the dead, summon demons and converse with gods, so long as there is a means by which these experiences can manifest. If you have no visionary ability, and fail to provide a communication device such as a pendulum or your best friend's body, the conversation is going to be pretty much one way.

No doubt some newcomers to magick will be disappointed to learn that magick will not allow you to grow an extra five inches (erm, in height), grant the ability to walk through walls or facilitate the turning of people into frogs.

But the 'physical' or 'real' world is simply one type of experience, and one means of materialisation amongst many. Dreaming is another type of experience. Whether you experience something in the 'real' world or in the 'dream' world makes no difference; the immediate effect of the experience is still the same. This may sound like a cop-out; but the ability to cure cancer, change peoples' minds and end the career of a murderer or rapist in the 'real' world isn't something to be sniffed at. You'll also be glad to hear that if there is one thing you will learn from magick, it is that what *can* manifest in the 'real' world is probably far beyond what you might expect.

The material manifestation of a desire is enough for a lot of magicians, to the extent that some will even say anything else simply isn't magick.

However, after your first successful act of magick, it is evident that magick offers…

REVELATION

The experience of a magical result will reveal something very odd about the nature of reality. This will have a transformative effect—your previous view of reality, and so yourself, must necessarily change as a result of that experience. It follows then that the more you do magick, the more you will encounter revelation, and the more you will be transformed.

It must be stressed that intellectual comprehension, or explanation, reveals or changes nothing. If you want to know the truth, you must experience it.

Magick is one way of experiencing truth.

CULTURE

It is often assumed that magick is simply a set of techniques. However, any set of techniques (or behavior) must necessarily include sociological and ethical implications, whether they are consciously addressed or not.

As such, magick is a culture. What form your magical culture takes depends on how you deal with the plethora of questions that must be confronted as a result of being able to bend reality, and the increased exposure to revelation, for example:

Do I help people with my magick? The whole community, close friends or just myself?

Do I evangelise magick, spouting its many virtues to all and sundry at every given opportunity, or do I practice it in secret?

Do I really want to maintain contact with my supposed best friends, and my loving family, if they fail to take my magick seriously, or superstitiously spurn me for practicing 'the Black Arts', without making the smallest amount of effort to try and accept me for *what I am*?

Should I curse the crap out of that man that gave me the beady eye, or his entire bloodline?

Should I find like-minded people for corroboration of experiences, the exchange of ideas, moral support and a goddamn fun and exciting time?

Should I only dress in black, wear a top hat and eyeliner, and call myself Dargon, High Priest of Voodoo', or do I exhibit some taste?[2]

Of course, this is by no means the full extent of the decisions you'll have to make as a budding magician.

THE CROSSROADS

If you do actually have a go at magick, sooner or later you'll come to the crossroads[3].

---

2. If you come across someone who claims magick is nothing more than a technology, ask him or her why they dress the way they do.

3. Actually, it's more of a T-junction, but that doesn't quite have the same ring to it, does it?

For a couple of years, my magical practice consisted of messing around with sigils (a very easy method of magick—see *Chapter 3 — Rub a sponge*). Eventually I reached a crossroads. The sign pointing to the left said: 'Quit dabbling with the occult, and actually do something "serious" with your life'; and to the right: 'Go all out, balls to the wall, and dedicate your life to chasing the ideal of being the greatest magician that has ever lived' (I have no idea what that means, but I do know that if you're not aiming to be the best you can be in any serious endeavor, you need to ask yourself why you're doing it).

I knew which road was right for me when I realised that I would undoubtedly come across events in my life that *I knew for a fact I could change for the better using magick.* If it looked like I might not be able to find the rent for next month by normal means, I knew I could do some magick to ensure it turned up. On a more serious note, what if someone in my family developed a life-threatening illness? How could I fail to resort to magick *knowing that it works*?

So there was no doubt about it—I couldn't leave magick alone.

That was a decade ago, and at this point in my life I no longer have an option of turning back. I've irrevocably transformed my reality. That might sound a little scary, and I suppose, at times, it is. But the happiness it brings is overwhelming (and thankfully more of an enduring feature).

Which brings me to a very important question: is magick for everyone?

A lot of magicians in the media spotlight have opted for magical evangelising. The attitude found in many 'next generation' occult blogs and books appears to assume that everyone would have a lot of fun if they just had a go. I mean, come on, it's a bit weird, but it's really easy and you'll have a good laugh, right?

When I first began dabbling, I thought a lot of what I read about the pitfalls of magick was a touch melodramatic. But that was ok, because I was a dabbler. When I became 'serious' about magick, I went out and found other 'serious' magicians. I then watched a few of them go barking mad.

Me, melodramatic?

Although the majority of magicians I've met haven't lost their minds, and have no doubt gained a certain amount of technical proficiency, very few have actually gone on to make any progress in terms of genuine magical development (by which I mean undergoing revelatory experiences at the metaphysical level of reality—see chapter 9). Magick requires a lot of hard work, and by its very nature, is difficult to understand.

We have now reached the point where I can safely be accused of being an elitist egomaniac. But tell me this: would a brain surgeon be an elitist egomaniac if he told you brain surgery is hard work and very difficult to understand? Do you think everyone has the aptitude and abilities required to perform brain surgery, safely and with any degree of success?

Magick isn't for everyone, but everyone *can* have a go. And just like brain surgery, things will get rather messy at times.

If you do decide to become a magician, remember: magick is about taking responsibility for your entire existence.

Are you up to it?

2. 'I Am External!'

Or:

'The Practice Of The Magical Diary'

Before we get down to the technical aspects of practicing magick, we must first introduce the use of the magical diary. It is traditional for the magician to write down every magical act, result and experience in the magical diary, which functions as a tool of encouragement, a scientific record and a means of magical integration.

When I first started magick, I really couldn't see the point. Considering the fact that as a magician I would be indulging in the bizarre and the weird, how likely is it that I'd forget an act of magick, its results or any mind-bending states of mind that might crop up? Furthermore, who cares if you forget a magical act or experience?

Of course, I'd already decided what the process of maintaining a magical diary had to offer. A couple of years down the line, realising my arrogance, I went and bought a suitably fancy journal, and got stuck into recording my magical activity.

For Shame

At first, I struggled to write everything down. This wasn't because I did so much magick, but because every time I opened my diary, the blank pages seemed to take pleasure in reminding me of how lazy I am.

I can say, without a shadow of a doubt, that if I did not keep a diary, my daily magical practice would tail off to perhaps once a week. Back then, maybe once a month.

Maintaining a magical diary actually makes you a more powerful and accomplished magician for this reason alone.

Read All About It

Besides its function as a goad, the diary is first and foremost a record. A written record of methods used, and results obtained, gives the magician the ability to improve future results, through the evaluation of those methods used in the past. It also renders visible any predilections for certain methods the magician might have, to be used either as an indicator of a potential specialisation, or as a sign that it is high time the magician expanded his or her repertoire and had a go at some other field of magical practice. It should also be noted that today's slightly insignificant but odd occurrence is tomorrow's mind-bending synchronicity; if you don't write it down, you may miss something *very important*.

SPECIAL

In terms of revelatory results, the diary serves a very special function.

The moment of experiencing revelation is a moment of experiencing truth. It makes no difference that once the revelation is over, it will eventually be succeeded by another revelation, for the words you use to describe any revelation are not the revelation itself. Truth is not knowable—it is *in the experience*.

This is best illustrated by someone tripping on LSD, who writes down what at the time is an extremely profound thought, only to discover, once sober, that it reads: 'I am external!' (and it's spelt incorrectly!). This sentence is far from profound; however, the experience that prompted the sentence certainly was.

Practicing magick will ensure your diary is dotted with many descriptions of such experiences; however, the aim of the game is to record the method used (if any), any pertinent conditions and a description of the state itself. Any incredible exclamations, such as 'I exist and do not exist simultaneously!' are to be recorded as symptomatic of the state, for example; 'whilst in this state I felt as though I both existed and did not exist at the same time.'

It is only through the description of the experience that we can come to understand that experience in a rational and useful manner. This is especially important when it comes to states of consciousness outside of the everyday trance.

Whilst you might develop a little mind control cult of your own by cheerfully informing everyone you meet 'I both exist and do not exist', you could only be accused of validating the existence of a state of consciousness where different rules of cognition apply, and providing a tried and tested method of experiencing that state, by refusing to give any validity to anything beyond the description of the experience itself.

This ensures that any such revelatory experience will not be left to gather dust in a folder marked 'obscure memory' in some dark recess of your mind, just like the time you took LSD and thought you understood the nature of reality. Indeed, your diary is the means of integrating such experiences, in a rational and sane manner, *into your life*.

It is true that a description is not the revelation itself. But the more revelations the magician experiences, and the richer the integration of those experiences, then the greater the flexibility of the habitual self, which in turn increases the probability of revelation occurring.

The practice of the magical diary is a catalyst for the transformation of the self.

EXERCISE 1

Write down every act of magick that you do, including the actual method used, and the results obtained.

Should you need one, here is an example of a diary entry, with a suggested format:

Date	*Time*	*Activity*
12/03/2008	14.21pm	Sigil method

Description
Created a sigil from the statement 'I will find my house keys'. Used concentration practice for gnosis. Found it difficult to forget the sigil afterwards, but this didn't take as long as last time.

A later diary entry might read:

13/03/2008	10.00am	Result from sigil on 12/03/2008

David just phoned—said he'd found a set of keys in the back of his car, and wondered if they were mine!

3. Rub A Sponge

Or:

'An Introduction To Magick'

Ask a magician to show you some magick and they will invariably show you how to make a sigil and 'charge' it[4].

This is known as sigil magick, it's incredibly easy and a good place for the beginner to start.

Pensioner Magick

The method of sigilisation consists of writing out a desire, omitting repeated letters then arranging the remainder into an arbitrary, abstract glyph. The magician then enters a state of great excitement or calm, by such methods as hyperventilation, meditation, flagellation or other pain inducing practices, dancing or entheogenic consumption; but the most popular method (for obvious reasons) is sex. At the

---

4. This is especially true of magicians who like to 'work alone'. Substitute 'charge' with 'have a wank' and you have their *raison d'etre* for remaining a solitary magician. Unless they like it when you watch.

peak of the altered state (this would be orgasm in the case of sex) the sigil is visualised or looked at, and then forgotten about.

Sometime after the act, the desire will manifest in the form of a synchronicity; so if your desire is 'I will get laid', you might find yourself hounded by a rotund monster at a party, who manages to corner you in the bathroom as your friends suddenly disappear.

Which brings me nicely to my next point (that last story never happened by the way). The gospel is: 'you get what you ask for'. So when you state your desire, do not say: 'I want to have sex'. You will simply find yourself working instantaneous magick (i.e. you will *want* to have sex). You need to state what you actually want to occur—like: 'I will win at the races'. It pays to be specific—for instance, 'I will have sex with a beautiful lady' would have been a more prudent example than 'I will get laid'.

EXERCISE 2

1.   Write down a desire.

2.   Create a sigil by omitting repeated letters, and then arranging the remainder into an arbitrary, abstract glyph.

3.   Masturbate.

4.   At the point of orgasm, visualise the sigil.

5.   Forget about it.

6.   Record the result in your diary.

How long it will take for the desire to manifest varies, but in my experience it's usually the next day or so.

And that's sigil magick!

Sex With Stationery

Everything I have said so far, however, is old hat. It is both amusing and very sad that no one has advanced the technique of sigilisation for almost a century.

Ask yourself: is there a secret mechanism to how magick works? Is there an unfathomable mystery hidden in the omission of repeated letters? Do you really believe in a Cosmic Committee for Correct Sigilisation Process?

Fuck the pen and paper.

Exercise 3

1. Think of something you want to occur. Mentally state it.

2. Now randomly create, using your imagination, an abstract glyph.

3. Decide that the glyph represents that statement. You have a sigil.

4. Go and 'charge' it, and wait for the result.

5. Record the outcome.

Finished? Now try this:

EXERCISE 4

1. Think of something you want, but make sure it is not the same desire you chose for *Exercise*

2. Mentally state it.

3. Remember the sigil you created for the first exercise? Visualize the same sigil, but now decide that the sigil represents *this* statement[5].

4. 'Charge' it and wait for the result.

5. Record the outcome.

Hmmm. Could this mean that what we use to represent our desire is arbitrary? And what does this say about the sigilisation process, and therefore magick itself?

SECRET CHIEF DANCING BEAR

It doesn't stop with glyphs; instead of a geometric doodle, you could use a number, or a combination of numbers. Or how about a word, nonsensical or otherwise?

What if we decide that a gesture represents your desire instead, like a wave of the hand? Or some other physical movement, like a dance? What if we decide that a certain dance means it will rain? You didn't think that really worked, did you?

---

5. Experience has shown that you can even get *someone else* to decide what your sigil means, and it still works. For more on this, investigate Remote Viewing.

EXERCISE 5

1. Open a book at a random page, and select the first three words from a random sentence.

2. Think of something you want to occur. Mentally state it.

3. Decide that those three words mean the same thing as your statement.

4. Masturbate, and at the point of orgasm, state those three words (whether mentally or out loud is up to you).

5. Record the result.

EXERCISE 6

1. Invent a dance (this can be as simple or as complex as you like—from a simple swaying motion to a full-blown routine).

2. Think of something you want to occur. Mentally state it.

3. Decide that the dance means the same thing as your statement (you can do this by saying your statement out loud just before step 4— this is sometimes known as a 'statement of intent').

4. Dance for ten minutes (or longer if you just can't help yourself).

5. Record the result.

White Van Man

Everything so far, although capable of delivering the goods, isn't really... exciting, is it? I mean, how corny is a rain dance? And after your 103rd sigil, the fun in imagining a couple of lines and a squiggle tends to wane a little, doesn't it?

What would happen if you stated your desire, then decided that whatever you did immediately after meant the same thing as the statement? What would happen if you could do anything, so long as you decide what it means, and you get your result regardless of method?

I'll tell you what—you become an artist. The emphasis shifts from anxiety over results to aesthetic consideration. What's stopping you? You can make your magick funny, witty or serious; ecstatic, absurd or deranged; profound or delirious.

Want to get laid? Why not cover yourself in jam and stick photos of attractive ladies or gentlemen to yourself?

Got a disease? Rub a sponge on the affected area, and then throw it off the top of a rollercoaster.

You can even make yourself rich by baking your credit card in a butter cream layer cake, *and* have a tasty treat to boot!

Exercise 7

1. Think of something that you want to occur.

2. Invent a ritual. This can be absolutely anything at all, but if you need somewhere to start, obtain items to use as representations of

the people or objects involved with your desired outcome, and act out that outcome. For instance, if your desire is 'S.M. will change her mind and decide to give me the pay rise I asked for', you might use an inflated balloon to represent her head, which you pop as a representation of her 'changing her mind'.

3. Decide that your ritual means the same thing as your statement (again, you can do this by simply saying your statement out loud before step 4).

4. Perform the ritual.

5. Record the experiment.

WHAT THE HELL DOES ALL OF THIS MEAN?

Let me tell you:

Magick is an art because it has no laws, only arbitrary aesthetics that dictate method (as long as you decide what an experience means, you can do anything, and it works).

Magick is a science because it has methodology (however arbitrary), with results that can be corroborated by peers through independent enquiry (just like you did, when you performed the exercises).

Magick is a culture because it has implicit social and ethical considerations (now you know that it works, what will you do with it? How has it changed your relationship with the world?)

Magicians (in their various guises) have always strived to understand 'how' magick works so that they might be able to do it 'correctly'. But whenever a magician wonders 'what is the correct method of getting a result?' they are falling victim to the fog of simplicity—because what you do, and the result you get, is your decision. There are no laws (unless you create them) and there are no secrets (unless you pretend).

So if magick is limited only by your imagination, just how beautiful will you make your magick? How ecstatic? Will magick be the most fun you've ever had in my life, or just the reason your wrist aches?

4. In The Beginning Was The Word

Or:
'How To Do Magick'

Here's a fundamental instruction in performing any act of magick:

1. Decide what you want to occur.

2. Ensure that what you want to occur has a means of manifestation.

3. Choose an experience.

4. Decide that the experience means the same thing as what you want to occur.

5. Perform the act/undergo the experience.

6. Result.

Examples of specific magical acts, such as sigilisation, divination, sympathetic magick, possession, evocation and other unspeakable depravities, will be given in the following chapters, all within the glorious context of this arbitrary outline.

5. Method To The Madness

'The Fallacy Of Magical Law'

Arbitrary magical methods (such as sigilisa-tion) are frequently mistaken for absolute magical laws. As I have already outlined in chapter 3, it must be stressed that no method or technique is essential to magick.

In this chapter, I will discuss four common methods that are frequently mistaken for magical laws. However, as arbitrary methods, we are not to regard them as superfluous or useless; rather, they are to be considered aesthetically. How much fun can you get out of using them? As 'game rules', how well do they promote or encourage magical invention?

The Sympathetic Method

From cave paintings of a successful hunt to your ex's head on a dartboard, the belief in 'like causing like' is perhaps as old as Man himself. Sympathetic magick is wonderful for encouraging or developing magical innovation. For instance, if you wanted to get rid of your boss, do you acquire a set of action figures and play out an office drama of what you want to happen? Or do you draw a little picture of him, chew it up and spit it out of your office window?

To be crude, it is true that 'like causes like', but it is also true that 'unlike causes like'. Consider the use of the nonsensical sigil as outlined in chapter 3. It is painfully obvious, even after the most cursory consideration of the concept of similarity, that to equate two things is a decision made by the magician. Do you think there is a Universal Similarity Department, run by a crack team of elemental inspectors, who will descend upon the doodle of your boss to measure how well you've captured his likeness?

Just as similarity is a decision, so is the meaning of an event. Whether it's playing with action men, or slapping yourself on the forehead with a banana, if you decide the experience means your boss will bugger off, then he will. You just need to make the decision, and perform the action.

A magical act does not *need* to be sympathetic to the desired result in order for it to work.

THE MAGICAL LINK METHOD

If you are going to be performing an act of magick that involves working directly on a person, then traditionally you are going to need what is commonly referred to as a magical link. This takes the form of some kind of genetic material (such as hair, blood or nail clippings) or an object that belongs to that person (such as a toothbrush or item of jewellery). Alternatively, you can create an object within a ritual that can then be put into contact with the person, such as a powder sprinkled across his or her path (commonly used in African/Caribbean sorcery) or in the form of a gift, such as a soft toy. It is often stated that you cannot work effective magick without the magical link.

But isn't it possible to work magick on a person, say with a sigil, just by writing his or her name? And what about the example used previously under the sympathetic method, where a picture is drawn of a person?

The truth is, with magick, you get what you ask for. If you know someone's name, and include it in your stated desire, such as 'Mary Higginbottom will be cured of her chicken pox', you will get that result.

The trouble comes when you consider the fact that there is more than one Mary Higginbottom in the world. Granted, it isn't very likely that you'll suddenly come across a different Mary Higginbottom who has just recovered from chicken pox, and it is also true that a little tweaking of the statement of intent, such as including her address, will ensure a better result. However, the traditional magical link does avoid writer's cramp, and is also indispensable when it comes to working accurate magick on someone you do not know (for instance, to affect a thief that regularly steals cash out of a shop register, you could leave a ritually 'charged' coin or banknote in the till, to form the link for the desired magical result).

Yes, you can have a traditional magical link, but it only serves as part of an accurate magical decision. Whether a part of that magical decision involves a six page physical description of a person, a very bad likeness in biro, or a toenail clipping is immaterial, so long as you remember you will get exactly what you have asked for.

A magical act does not *need* a traditional magical link in order to have an effect on a person.

THE GNOSIS METHOD

A very recent 'indispensable' magical technique to hit the occult scene is the idea of gnosis. First mentioned in *Liber Null*, gnosis is used to describe any altered state of consciousness induced through a wide variety of activities (see chapter 3 for a list of these activities).

It is true that gnosis works as a magical technique, with many reasons given for its efficacy, from allowing a desire to be 'buried' within the subconscious, which is (apparently) where a desire needs to go in order to bear fruit; all the way to increasing the amount of energy available to 'put into' a desire, thereby enhancing its manifestation.

However, although gnosis is often considered common to all magical traditions, many African/Caribbean approaches (such as Quimbanda) do not use altered states of consciousness[6]

6. Possession does not require the person being possessed, or 'the horse', to enter a trance, although being possessed is cer-

in order to work magick. Of course, we don't need to examine such traditions for evidence of the arbitrary nature of gnosis; we simply need to consider the efficacy of the sympathetic method.

Gnosis is not necessary for magick, but it is one method. So how might we best understand gnosis alongside other methods that do not use altered states of consciousness?

It goes without saying that gnosis can be used in your magick as part of a chosen aesthetic, such as the subconscious or energy models mentioned above. Like any other magical act, it does what you decide it does within the ritual.

But it is blindingly obvious that you can enter an altered state, 'charge' a sigil, and get a result, without even being aware of any explanation, or working within an aesthetic such as the subconscious or energy models.

Independent from artistic considerations then, let's consider what is actually experienced during a ritual using gnosis.

Gnosis, or an altered state of consciousness, only becomes part of a magical act at the moment you undergo the experience you have decided means the same thing as your desire. In other words, at the moment you experience the visualisation of the sigil or the chosen action.

What occurs here is exactly the same as what occurs during sympathetic magick; you decide what an experience will mean, then you undergo that experience.

---

tainly a different state of consciousness (if the horse is conscious at all).

There is no difference between the experience of a visualised sigil, and the experience of sticking pins in a doll, if you have decided they both mean the same thing. However, you don't need gnosis to make the doll work.

So why do you need gnosis to work a sigil?

Actually it isn't necessary, but when you first start practicing magick, you need a little help overcoming a mental habit that very rarely poses a problem when performing a physical action. If you create a sigil and visualise it, you will discover that you must make an effort to resist desiring the outcome of the visualisation. It is very easy to change the experience of visualising the sigil into a different experience from the one previously decided.

As an example, say you've created a sigil that means: 'I will win some money'.

Instead of undergoing this experience: I will win some money (which is what the experience of your visualised sigil means), you undergo this experience: I hope this sigil works. Beginners are rarely aware that they are deciding to experience the latter instead of the former, and that the key to magick lies in *what you experience*.

Hoping a sigil works is still an act of magick—it just has instantaneous results (i.e. you experience the hope that your sigil works).

Gnosis, as part of a magical process, can be seen as an environment conducive to experiencing mental phenomena in exactly the same way as physical phenomena, with the same mental attitude, say, of moving your legs, or throwing a ball.

In light of the above, it makes sense that gnosis is usually described as a state of 'being without desire'.

Gnosis helps you experience your chosen decision, but gnosis is not necessary in order to experience that decision.

A magical act does not *need* gnosis in order to work.

THE AMNESIA METHOD

This method usually goes hand in hand with sigilisation. After the act, you make a willed effort to forget the act, and the sigil.

In the subconscious aesthetic, this ensures the desire remains in the subconscious, where it will come to fruition.

This is the only explanation I've ever come across for the amnesia method, but even if you are not working with the subconscious aesthetic, experience has shown that forgetting your magical act helps to ensure your desire will manifest.

Many of the criticisms made earlier concerning gnosis are applicable here. Although amnesia is helpful, especially for the beginner, it is not essential in making your magick work, and is usually not applicable when you've used a method that rests solely on a physical experience, such as the sympathetic approach.

What happens when you remember an act of magick?

Remembering a magical act or experience is similar to the beginner visualising a sigil without gnosis. You will tend to create an instant magical result: you hope your magick works.

You revert from your original experience (the sigil or act, meaning 'I will win some money') to the experience: 'I hope I win some money' or 'I hope my magick works'.

To hope or wish is the qualification that you do not have what you want. You cannot have your chosen experience, and the unintentional experience (which is the desire for your chosen experience), at the same time. When you desire, you are making a magical decision and so an instant magical result, although, as a beginner, you are unaware that you are doing so.

With time and practice, it will become possible to remember the magical act without working magick against yourself. Of course, it is a lot harder to desire the outcome of a magical act when the memory of *what you actually did* makes you wet yourself with laughter.

A magical act does not *need* to be forgotten in order for it to work.

OK...

So now we know that some of the more popular 'magical laws' are not essential to performing an act of magick. In order to understand how these 'magical laws' fit in with the instruction given in chapter 4, over the next page there's a table with examples of how you might perform a magical act to get your boss to resign, using the arbitrary methods we've discussed.

So: what are you waiting for?

EXERCISE 8

1. Bearing the outline in mind, create and per-
    form four rituals using the first four methods
    given in the table overleaf, without perform-
    ing the fifth.

2. Record the results.

Outline	Sympathetic method	Gnosis / sigil method
1. Decide what you want to occur.	My manager will resign	My manager will resign
2. Ensure that what you want to occur has a means of manifestation.	I do have a manager and there is the possibility for him to resign.	I do have a manager and there is the possibility for him to resign.
3. Choose an experience.	Chewing up a picture of my manager and spitting it out of the window	The visualisation of an abstract glyph
4. Decide that the experience means the same thing as what you want to occur.	Chewing up a picture of my manager and spitting it out of the window means my manager will resign	The writing out of step 1, the removal of repeating letters and the construction of an abstract glyph out of what remains (alternatively, you could just decide any abstract glyph means the same thing as step 1)
5. Perform the act/undergo the experience.	Chew up a picture of your manager and spit it out of the window	While in gnosis, visualise the sigil then block all memory of the sigil out of your mind until he's buggered off.
6. Result.	Within a day/week/month?	Within a day/week/month?

Magical link method	Nonsensical magical act	The magical act of desiring
My manager will resign	My manager will resign	I hope my manager will resign.
I do have a manager and there is the possibility for him to resign.	I do have a manager and there is the possibility for him to resign.	I do have a manager and there is the possibility for him to resign.
Throwing my manager's pen out of the window	Tying a shoe to a tree, running round it three times, then spitting on it	My immediate experience
Throwing my manager's pen, which is magically linked to him, out of the office window means my manager will resign	Tying a shoe to a tree, running round it three times, then spitting on it, means my manager will resign	What I am experiencing now means I hope my manager will resign
Throw your manager's pen out of the window	Tie your shoe to a tree, run round it three times and then spit on it	This was already happening at step 2; it is due to this that it is difficult to realise that being in a state of desire is an act of magick —with an instantaneous result
Within a day/week/month?	Within a day/week/month?	The result has already manifested

6. A Model Magician

Or:
'How To Believe'

A popular aesthetic in occultism at the moment is science. Making magick look scientific is easy:

1. Come up with an explanation for how magick works and call it 'a model' or 'theory' (for instance, Chaos Magic becomes Chaos Magic Theory, or the belief in spirits is referred to as 'the Spirit Model').

2. Abbreviate the name of your explanation, and where possible any techniques or methods too (for instance, Chaos Magic Theory becomes CMT).

3. Describe your explanation or model using algebra and mathematics.

4. Reference scientific principles from a branch of science (such as quantum mechanics) in your rituals.

5. Describe magick using scientific jargon and terminology (magick is 'a technology', or an act of 'meta-programming').

There are many more methods, such as referring to magical texts as 'papers', but I'm sure you can come up with further examples should you wish to work with the scientific aesthetic.

Remember: the scientific aesthetic is not the same thing as the scientific method. As stated earlier, we can apply the scientific method to magick (and it must be applied for it to be science), but the scientific method is not the current culture of science. Dressing in a white lab coat, using specialist jargon to describe the scientific method, or investing belief in the current favourite theory or model for quantum effects, does not make you a scientist.

However, just because something is an aesthetic doesn't mean it is 'wrong' or useless. The question isn't 'is it correct?' but 'does making my magick look "scientific" float my boat?'

Culture Vulture

Beyond culture then, to what extent are explanations or models useful for the magician?

It has often been assumed that working with different models of magick is beneficial to the magician, as it demonstrates the arbitrary nature of any viewpoint, and allows the magician to use belief as a tool for creating magical effects. This is referred to as 'belief shifting'.

However, there is a big difference between *using* a belief or model, and adopting a belief as an explanation.

Explanation provides an intellectual understanding of a subject. It changes nothing but the intellectual viewpoint of the person adopting the explanation. This is evident by the ease at which you can *change your mind* and adopt a new explanation, and the reason why so many people talk about conditioning and yet act exactly the same as everyone else.

Preferring one explanation to another for a couple of weeks is not belief shifting.

If you wish to change your experience or viewpoint, then you need to actually experience a different viewpoint or model, as an aesthetic within a magical act.

For a model to be of any use at all it must cease being an explanation and become an actual event. Chapter 4 tells you how to do this in terms of the arbitrary ritual outline, but a much simpler way is literally to say that if you want to make an idea or belief true, you need simply to act on it.

The act is the experience of the belief. The act makes the belief true.

Just for clarification, the act is steps 3 to 5 of the ritual outline.

Of course, you may protest that you don't deliberately decide that an action means the same thing as your belief, nor do you ponder what experience you are going to use, when you perform an action. You just do it.

This is true, and this is where the ritual outline becomes cumbersome and largely unnecessary beyond making the magical act explicit.

A WONDERFUL WORLD

If all you need to do is act on a belief to make it true, then if you want to live in a happy, wonderful world, all you need to do is *act* like you live in a happy, wonderful world. This can be anything from a full-blown ritual act to something as simple as telling yourself the world is a fun, good place to be.

Of course, just saying this once won't change much—try it, and see how fast you revert back to thinking and acting as if the world *isn't* a happy, wonderful place. In order to work magick on the self effectively you must replace the habitual magick that you do everyday with *new* habitual magick. This means repetition.

Although I've said that all you need to do to make a belief true is to act on it, please do not think that if you believe you can fly, then jumping off a tall building will make it so; remember step 2 of the ritual outline. Ensure there is a means of manifestation for the belief. For a belief to manifest in the material world, it must be within the game rules of the material world. Humans do not fly.

Humans can, however, remake themselves as they see fit. It's possible to ditch a crappy world view for a good one; swap depression for joy; pessimism for optimism; or anxiety for peace.

EXERCISE 9

1. Tell yourself you are stupid, ugly, and no one likes you.

2. Do it everyday for two weeks.

3. Record the results.

EXERCISE 10

1. Tell yourself you are intelligent, attractive and everyone loves you.

2. Do it everyday for two weeks.

3. Record the results.

Compare the results from exercise 9 with those of exercise 10. Choose one for life.

BUT I LIKE ARGUING DOWN THE PUB

If your reality rests solely on the magical act, and so you can change your experience as you see fit, then any viewpoint or belief is *true* at the moment you experience it.

To argue about 'how magick actually works', as if the truth is not in the experience itself, is indicative of a failure to understand magick.

An example of this is the ubiquitous debate on the occult scene as to the true nature of spirits, usually taking the form of a discussion around 'are they real', versus 'are they just amplified parts of my psychology?' If you decide to interact with a god and do so, but then go down the pub to tell your friends you believe gods are simply parts of your personality, you have failed to understand that the truth is in the experience. You may believe gods are part of your psychology, but belief only becomes genuine *when it is experienced*.

If you want to work with the different parts of your psyche, then take up psychotherapy and work with them. This is still magick—you have chosen a belief and acted upon it. This isn't an argument for a preferred model, but an emphasis on experiencing belief, whatever that belief may be. Don't work with a spirit, and then dismiss the truth of your experience and deny the fact that *your reality is your decision*, by claiming spirits are something other than spirits.

EXERCISE 11

1. Do not wait for the 'correct' explanation before doing any magick.

2. Whether in a ritual space or not, choose a belief, and act on it (Choose a belief that doesn't necessitate hurting or killing anyone; believing that your mother has been replaced by an alien bent on world domination also isn't very healthy. A good example might be deciding to believe in God, and acting on it by going to church or praying everyday).

3. Change your beliefs frequently (for instance, once you do believe in God, become a rational Buddhist and take up Vipassana).

7. What's In A Name?

Or:

'Magical Mottos And Oaths'

One of the most misunderstood and largely undervalued magical acts is the adoption of a magical name, as is customary in the Western tradition of magick. In the past this has been taken very seriously by secret magical societies, as it sometimes is today, but usually for the wrong reasons. It is common to be attracted to magick simply for the fun of magical culture—dressing up in extravagant robes, speaking archaic barbarous words in a booming voice, meeting up in dark, secret places with fellow conspirators against the norm, and announcing yourself as Prometheon the Grand Arch Master of the Pyramid. Magick attracts the pretentious like flies to shit, and Lord knows there are too many ham magicians out there who take themselves too damn seriously.

With postmodernism came Chaos Magic and Discordianism, and the advent of the humorous magical name—after all, magick doesn't need to be serious in order for it to work, does it? Prometheon became Potatoface the Slowly Reclining, and magick became a bit of a laugh. Magick also attracts yahoos like flies to shit, and there are too many ham magicians out there who think themselves too damn funny.

Get Over It

So is the magical name more than just a device for hamming it up?

Once we get past the allure of magical culture, a magical name or motto serves a very specific and irrefutable magical function, and the funny or serious nature of a name bears this out. The magical name is the sum of the magician's approach, understanding and experience of magick. It is impossible for it to be anything else.

At first, when magick is novel and fun, a name may be chosen that sounds whacky or outrageous, like Frater Fabulous or Soror Sandwichmaster[7]. Or perhaps it may be recognised early on that magick is a developmental process, and so a name that acknowledges the anticipation of the arrival of a truly magical identity is adopted—like Frater Void or Soror Unnamed. It may be that magick is taken very seriously indeed and a name is created using Qaballah—this will inevitably produce a name reminiscent of those favoured by Victorian secret societies, like Frater Yechidah or Soror I.A.O.

7. *Frater* and *Soror* are Latin for 'Brother' and 'Sister' respectively.

DEED POLL

I performed an act of magick to generate my first magical name, which isn't surprising considering I was of the opinion that magick should be divorced from conscious deliberation. The result was my appearance in a friend's dream, holding what she described as a 'festooned stick'. I took the name Festoon—suitably strange, and indicative of the fact that I wasn't yet aware of my true magical nature —I was covered, or 'festooned', with my everyday personality, so to speak.

As my approach to magick changed and my experience deepened, so too did my name and its meaning. My magical motto became much more specific to my emerging nature, as I discovered my purpose in life in light of a series of intense Holy Guardian Angel workings (see chapter 14). But this isn't always the case with every magician—some magicians start off serious, only to lighten up and adopt a more relaxed and fun approach to magick. Some magicians don't change their approach at all and remain with the same persona for their entire magical career. Some magical orders require a change of magical name with each grade attained, but this doesn't necessarily indicate a revolution in magical attitude or approach. Whatever the circumstances of your adopted magical persona, there is no escaping the fact that the magical name determines who you are as a magician, and it should at least be acknowledged that the identity you have chosen is an act of magick preformed on the self.

If you choose a superficial and bonkers magical name, what does that say about your attitude to magick in general? Do you think this approach is indicative of the fact you're only dabbling with magick?

If you choose an intellectual or symbolically complex magical name, do you think perhaps your expectations of magick are woefully off the mark? Are you being pretentious?

How do you see yourself developing in a magical sense? Do you have a plan, and what name might express this aspiration best?

EXERCISE 12

1. Devise and adopt a magical name you are comfortable with, using the means you find most suitable.

2. Once created, investigate what the name says about your approach, perception and understanding of magick. Record the results from adopting this name (this will be ongoing).

3. Revise your magical name as and when necessary.

THE MAGICAL OATH

Picture the scene: a shadowy chamber lit by candlelight, swirling incense smoke, a robed and hooded assembly, the glint of sharp steel as a blade is pressed against the throat of a bound and naked young man. The subject of this terrible ordeal repeats the words spoken to him by the looming figure holding the dagger, swearing by his very soul to keep silent about the group's activities and the identities of its members, over penalty of unspeakable torture and death.

Six months later, the young man receives an e-mail informing him he can no longer come to the pub with the Order of the Massive Serpent, because he posted one of their rituals on an internet site without asking first.

Torture and death indeed.

POKED WITH A STICK

You could be forgiven for thinking that the above is just one more example of the predictable histrionics of the magical scene—a lofty, portentous oath is sworn in blood only to result in no longer being friends.

However, the magical oath is generally just as much misunderstood and undervalued as the magical name. While it is true that to all appearances the actuality of breaking the typical occult group oath results in nothing like the punishments promised, it should be borne in mind that a magical oath engenders a magical result. It is foolish to take the apparent profane events surrounding the breaking of a magical oath as either the success or failure of the oath, if those events are not *exactly what were asked for.*

The magical oath binds the magician to a chosen future—and the truly magical oath of a group or order will have the exact magical consequences it states, regardless of the apparent 'actual' events that occur when the oath is broken.

It cannot be stressed too strongly—be careful what you agree to, because just like the magical name, to take an oath is to perform an act of magick on yourself!

Debt

Of course, the magical oath can be taken for all kinds of reasons, not just group affiliation. You can swear to stop certain habits and implement new ones; to highly achieve at an event or as the result of a certain activity; to radically alter your world view; or to devote your life to a specific cause.

When I was a young and naïve magician I attempted and failed to make magick a part of my day-to-day life to such an embarrassing extent that I decided to take a magical oath to remedy the situation. Just like magical names, the efficacy of an oath is not dependent on how humorous, pretentious or cheesy the magician might be.

Still very much seduced by turn-of-the-twentieth-century magical culture, I signed my name in a suitably dramatic fashion to the following oath as recorded in my magical diary:

> *I solemnly swear to I.A.O. that I will attain to Godhead; I further put myself at the disposal of the Secret Chiefs, and swear to play my part in the initiation of mankind. Witness my hand:*
> *[Signed A. Chapman]*

A few good joints later and the oath was conveniently forgotten. Imagine my surprise almost a decade later when the 'Secret Chiefs' actually came to collect on my promise...

EXERCISE 13

1. Very carefully consider devising and signing a magical oath. The oath can be as cheesy, humorous, pretentious or as tasteful as you like. However, *be flippant at your own risk*.

2. Record the results.

8. GOT YOUR NUMBER

OR:

THE QUALITATIVE PRACTICALITY OF SYMBOLISM IN RITUAL

Before the advent of Chaos Magic, the Western magician was expected to study and memorise a vast symbolic language composed from various magical sources—such as the Egyptian, Hermetic and Alchemical schools—before being taught any practical magick. This tended to make magick a somewhat intellectual pursuit within many of the Victorian magical orders, with the majority of classical practitioners appearing mostly all mouth and no trousers.

After Chaos Magic, with the bare bones of practical sorcery made available in any good bookshop and presented in a manner any half-wit could implement, the emphasis previously placed on symbolism was left looking rather misplaced. For example, why bother memorising the various columns of Crowley's 777 before even attempting some actual magick, when most 'real world' magical results can be gained through the use of a simple sigil?

Bend Over

Nothing teaches quite like direct experience. The sooner the magician gets down to practicing magick, no matter how easy, boring or simple the technique employed, the better. Chaos Magic has certainly done the Western magical world a great service in this respect. But as we know, what is experienced during ritual is our decision—so what might it mean to employ a complex symbolism during the ritual act? Beyond perhaps adding a certain aesthetic, or an element of fun, might the use of symbolism serve a practical purpose?

Consider a ritual to evoke an entity. True enough, given enough practice we can perform any designated action in order to engender the required result (see chapter 11 for more on this). But what if, as well as performing the designated action (say, reciting barbarous words), we were to employ a magical phallic wand specially consecrated to manifest entities, with which we draw the entities seal? And what if incense is burnt that is deemed commensurate with the nature of the entity being summoned?

Therefore as well as the original action to evoke the entity, we have a further two levels of complexity in the operation. If we consider the fact that a magical result is a synchronicity, or the occurrence of two events with the same meaning, does it not follow that the complexity of the meaning of the outcome will reflect the complexity of the meaning involved in the ritual?

In other words, more meaning in equals more meaning out!

FILTHY RICH

It cannot be made too explicit that the application of complex symbolism does not mean an increase in quantitative results, but an increase in the quality of the result. The quantification of magick can only be entertained when causality is still considered adequate as a description of the magical act (we'll explore this in greater detail in chapter 14). With a quantitative approach to magick, the simple sigil engenders the same number of results as the overblown symbolic rite—i.e. one! But if we consider the two magical acts in a qualitative sense, the symbolic rite creates a more meaningful result due to the richness of the meaning employed during the ritual.

However, the novice must not try and run before he or she can walk. It is essential during a ritual that every element of the magical act has a clear purpose and a reason for doing it. It is better to decide what one action means and undergo that experience, than to attempt to employ a thousand symbols not fully understood and end up confused in the middle of a cumbersome and overly cerebral rite.

MAGICAL LANGUAGE

So where might we begin in order to learn this 'magical language' for use in the magical act? How are we to make sense of so many symbols from so many traditions?

If we were to accept that the universe is composed solely of ideas, and that the most elementary expression of an idea, and its relationship with other any other idea, is mathematical in nature, would it not be possible to attribute any phenomena whatsoever to number?

If it were really possible to attribute every phenomenon or every symbol to a number, we could develop not only a mnemonic system beyond parallel, but also an intuitive, coherent means of understanding every symbol in relation to every other.

The symbolic complexity of a ritual would then not only be a matter of the material symbols employed during ritual, but on the breadth and depth of the magician's symbolic association developed by using such a numerical system as outlined above.

Thankfully for us such a system already exists, and seems to have existed in various cultures around the world for millennia. Today we know it as the Qaballah.

Exercise 14

1. Choose a Qaballah: Hebrew, Greek, Latin, English, GoN, etc, purchase a good book on the subject and memorise the alphabet with its numerical values.

2. Develop a 'book of numbers': Write down every number from 0 to 1,000. Work out the numerical value of all of the ideas that are important to you (using the Qaballah you have

chosen), and write them next to the corresponding number. Add words as and when necessary.

3.   Study the Tree of Life, and work out where
each word in your 'book of numbers' belongs.

4.   Study all possible mathematical relationships,
and ascertain what these relationships mean
for the ideas to which you apply them.

5.   Classify every phenomenon you experience in
terms of the Tree, until it is habitual.

EXERCISE 15

1.   Devise a simple ritual for a specific result. Perform it and record the results.

2.   Devise a ritual with a similar result as number
1 above, but this time employ a rich symbolism, such as the use of appropriate incense,
colour schemes, robes, candles, sounds, music,
food, drink, physical acts, etc. Record the results.

3.   Compare and record any differences between
the results for 1 and 2.

9. The World As We Know It

Or:

'The Available Means Of Manifestation'

In chapter 1, I stated that what can be experienced through magick is limited only by your imagination, but how you experience a magical result is limited by the available means of manifestation.

The available means of manifestation is the world as we know it and a bit more besides.

We tend to consider the sensations that make up our five senses as 'reality'. This is where all the action takes place, and this is where we encounter our most visceral experiences. Of course, there are also the mental and emotional categories or levels of experience, but as these are private events and exempt from consensual corroboration, they are often considered less 'real' (and so less important) than the physical world. Last and certainly least in our descending scale of consensual reality comes dreaming—not only is this subjective, but it actually occurs in a different state of consciousness and exhibits laws of an order completely different to those experienced during the waking state, or what we call 'normal life'.

The idea that some experiences are more valid or 'real' than others sneaked into Western culture a few centuries ago with the advent of Rationalism. Once reason had become the highest authority (as opposed to metaphysical or divine experience) we were left with no option but to consider anything not easily rationalised as delusional or hallucinatory. In other words, our world became limited to only those experiences immediately identifiable as belonging to either the rational, emotional or physical levels of experience.

Considering the fact that we as a culture have effectively 'tuned out' any type of experience not considered 'real' for the past three hundred years, it should come as no surprise that our magical culture has followed suit. The sole criterion of today's effective 'practical' magick is the occurrence of a quantitative result: did the magical act cause a real world material event to occur? Yes or no?

MENTAL

However, we need only consider what actually occurs during mental/emotional/dream experience to see that our current reductionist material view of reality is confused.

A dream is only considered illusory once the experience is over and we return to the 'real world', but this does not mean the actual experience of the dream is any less genuine whilst it is occurring. Would it not be silly to believe a thought illusory because it isn't an emotion? Are we not committing the same fallacy when we regard all other levels of experience in light of the physical level?

Whereas the average westerner is conditioned to ignore and dismiss various parts of his or her experience, the magician actively adopts an inclusive exploratory approach to the various levels of his or her being through personal, direct experience. It should come as no surprise that the practice of magick will inevitably lead to the types of experience the average westerner would consider fantastic, simply because that experience belongs to part of the means of manifestation not normally considered real.

LOW DOWN

So far we have categorised experience as follows: physical, emotional, mental, and dream. With dream we can also include the imagination, as both types of experience share fundamental characteristics, and revert to the traditional heading for this category, which is 'astral'.

There are also another three planes we can add to the list, described in more or less every magical tradition the world over, but whose existence can easily be corroborated through certain practices: these are the etheric, metaphysical and non-dual planes. Before we explore these however, let's take a closer look at the astral.

ASTRAL

Most human beings are intimate with the physical, emotional and mental realms on a daily basis, and generally their understanding of these levels is much more advanced than their understanding of the astral. While it is true that our imagination is more or less in constant use with daydreaming, planning and fantasising, the attitude of seeing the imagination as an illusory function of the mind, and dream as a peculiarity of sleep, has stunted our exploration of the astral realm as a plane with its own specific laws, flora and fauna.

The astral realm can be fully accessed in two ways: lucid dreaming and astral projection. The first method involves the cultivation of self-consciousness during dreaming, whereas the second method requires the cultivation of dreaming whilst awake. Whichever technique is used, it should be borne in mind that a realm is being explored complete with its own intelligent inhabitants, peculiar rules and specific dangers. Remember: just because it is the astral realm, it doesn't mean the experience is illusory.

If you wish to experience the astral realm via lucid dreaming, try the following:

EXERCISE 16

1. Keep a dream diary. As soon as you wake up, write down everything you can remember about your dreams. If initially you fail to recall anything it is important you still attempt the

exercise every morning. Eventually recall will become easier and the ability to remember all your dreams without the use of the diary can be developed through perseverance. Record any results.

2. On a daily basis and during waking hours, attempt to change the colour of the floor you are standing on through will power alone. Eventually this should establish itself as a habit that will be expressed whilst dreaming, triggering lucidity. Record your results.

3. Perform an act of magick to experience a lucid dream. Record the results.

4. Once lucidity is established, it may prove difficult to prevent the dream from dissipating. The only solution to this is repetition. However, with practice, lucid dreaming will allow you to travel in your astral body to wherever you might wish to go on the astral plane—you can construct temples and sacred spaces, evoke entities and experiment with shape changing. But be warned: if you don't have a good banishing ritual (see chapter 11) under your belt or a means of protection, you are leaving yourself wide open to astral attack. As always, record your results.

If you wish to experience the astral plane through astral projection, try the following:

Exercise 17

1. Lie down and relax.

2. Become aware of your imaginary body. Although you are essentially imagining the body, there should be an element of allowing the sensations of the astral body to arise of their own accord.

3. Now move around in your imagined form, see with your imaginary eyes, hear with your imaginary ears, etc. For some, astral travel comes easy, but for a lot of people it can be quite difficult. If at this point you are struggling to 'leave' the physical body and sense with your imaginary senses, there is only one possible course of action—practice! Some find it useful to move a physical limb, remember what the physical sensation felt like, and then use that memory as a basis for moving the corresponding astral limb, as an exercise in slowly building up the astral form. However I very much believe in simply repeating the above exercise —usually, the 'knack' is suddenly gained and the problems vanish, much like with lucid dreaming. Keep in mind that you are trying to access something that is already there, which you already experience every night.

4. Explore! However, be cautious—not all astral beings are who they say they are, and not all beings mean well. Again, it is prudent to have mastered a good banishing ritual. If you wish to gain a greater understanding of a certain

idea, travel to its astral abode. For instance, if you wish to explore Malkuth on the Tree of Life, you can create a door with the necessary attributes (such as the appropriate colour, symbol, and material peculiar to Malkuth) to take you there.

5. Be sure to return the astral body to the physical body at the end of the practice—who knows what might happen to it left unattended...

ETHERIC

Residing between the physical and emotional levels of experience, the etheric level is the realm of subtle energetics, and includes the experience known as *prana* in India, *chi* in china, *ki* in Korea and Japan, Wilhelm Reich's *orgone*, Yoruban *ashe*, *ka* of the Egyptians, the Polynesian *mana*, *nefesh* of Judaism, and the Aboriginal *maban* (this is of course just a small selection of traditional examples of this phenomenon). We have taken the title for this category from the European alchemical name for the experience, which is *ether*.

Ether can be considered the 'life force' or the fundamental energy inherent in all things, although it should not be confused with consciousness itself. Traditionally ether is intrinsically linked with the breath, and most traditions teach breathing exercises as a means of accessing this experience, as well as the use of specific postures. Ether is used for healing in practices such as Reiki or in the 'laying on of hands', and can be used to cause injury through internal martial arts such as Ba Gua, Tai Chi and Hsing Yi.

However, perhaps the most powerful application of ether is as a means of accessing the metaphysical plane (see below). In many etheric traditions, such as kundalini or kriya yoga, the etheric force is often depicted as a snake or serpent residing at the bottom of the spine, which through a combination of breathing and posture is induced to travel up the body, awakening various magical powers as it goes, until it reaches its destination just above the crown of the head to result in a metaphysical experience.

Ether can be considered the interface between the body and the mind. We can influence ether through visualisation and intent, which in turn influences the body. Hence many etheric arts appear to those that have never experienced the etheric as simple visualisation exercises, such as the use of imagined symbols in reiki, or visualising the arms as made of iron in Hsing Yi, or the hundreds of variant chakra or energy centre systems found in Hinduism and Tantra. Experience of the etheric is essential before these techniques can be understood and practiced properly.

Given enough practice we can also experience the etheric body, but bear in mind that the astral and etheric bodies are often confused. Whereas the astral body inhabits the astral plane, which is unmistakably a unique environment, the etheric body seems to overlap both the astral and physical worlds. The transition to the etheric body can be quite an intense 'physical' experience, usually involving a great buzzing sensation that can be quite unpleasant. Generally, accounts of out of body experiences (OBEs) are usually describing experience of the etheric plane, although many amateurs will describe OBEs as astral projection.

In my experience and that of others, accessing the etheric body is much more of a challenge than accessing the astral form. Although intense meditative practice can help with this, the following four exercises have proven the most effective at furnishing experience of the etheric, if not a full-blown OBE experience:

EXERCISE 18

1. Sit in a relaxed, comfortable position with your back straight.

2. The following is one complete round of a basic pranayama exercise incorporating alternate nostril breathing:

3. Inhale through the left nostril, closing the right with the thumb, to the count of four.

4. Hold the breath, closing both nostrils, to the count of sixteen.

5. Exhale through the right nostril, closing the left with the ring and little fingers, to the count of eight.

6. Inhale through the right nostril, keeping the left nostril closed with the ring and little fingers, to the count of four.

7. Hold the breath, closing both nostrils, to the count of sixteen.

8. Exhale through the left nostril, keeping the right closed with the thumb, to the count of eight.

9. Start by practicing three rounds and build up slowly to twenty rounds. Once this exercise becomes easy, the count can be extended providing the ratio remains 2:8:4.

10. Record the results.

11. Investigate other pranayama and breath work exercises.

EXERCISE 19

1. Stand with feet shoulder width apart, back straight, with a slight bend to the knees. Relax the shoulders and let your arms hang by your side with a slight curve at the elbow. The inside of the arms should not be touching the sides of your body—imagine a tennis ball under each armpit to gauge the correct distance. The hands should be completely relaxed.

2. Stand in this position, without moving at all, for 15 minutes, eventually building up to 1 hour.

3. It is not essential to keep your awareness on the body during this exercise for it to work, and you can even watch television or listen to music should you feel bored. Sooner or later

persistent pains may develop in certain areas of the body during the practice. Classically these pains are considered etheric blockages that will eventually dissipate through continued practice, and so it is important to maintain the posture for the allocated time.

4. The results of this simple exercise can be quite astounding. Preliminary results are generally experienced in the hands first, and can be anything from the awareness of subtle sensations such as tingling, vibration, fullness, coldness or hotness, all the way to ether moving your limbs *of its own accord*. Whatever happens, remember to write it down.

EXERCISE 20

1. Take up kundalini yoga.

2. Record any results.

EXERCISE 21

1. Design an act of magick for experiencing ether / the etheric body / having an out of body experience.

2. Perform the rite and record the results (this exercise will work wonderfully in conjunction with one of the practices given above).

METAPHYSICAL

A metaphysic is simply a language for describing events at the profound or mystical level of experience, which *transcends but includes* the physical, etheric, emotional, mental and astral planes. Metaphysical experience falls into two main categories: states of absorption and stages of insight.

Techniques that engender states of absorption can be defined as the practice of reducing awareness to a single experience *whilst excluding all other experience*. Examples of this kind of practice are yogic concentration exercises, entheogenic consumption, sex, flagellation, breath work, dance, etc. States of absorption are usually referred to as trances, and are rather misleadingly called 'gnosis' in Chaos Magic. States of absorption are a key element of sigil magick (see chapter 3).

The specific characteristics of a state of absorption largely depend on expectations brought to the exercise used to induce the state. For instance, in Theravada Buddhism it is possible to practice and experience eight types of trance called Jhanas through concentration exercise. Similarly, if using breath work to enter trance from a rebirth perspective, the absorption state will predictably carry the characteristics of a traumatic experience. It's possible to induce any kind of experience with absorption states given enough practice and the use of the appropriate focus, and intense bliss, past life recall and visions are all possible. The fact that the magician becomes 'absorbed' in the exercise has fooled many into believing that absorption in an experience such as 'nothingness' or some other refined and subtle perception is the equivalent to experiencing the goal or end result of the metaphysical process, which as stated earlier is experienced in stages as opposed to being a state.

Techniques that initiate stages of insight can be defined as the practice of maintaining an awareness of the immediate sensations that make up reality whilst allowing those sensations to arise and pass away of their own accord. Rather than becoming absorbed in such a practice, the continued observation of reality in the present begins a cycle of progressive insight into the nature of reality, with recognisable and predictable stages and a definite end result, sometimes referred to as enlightenment or illumination. This is the Great Work of magick. Due to the tendency of the mind to wander, a degree of skill in concentration is necessary to perform insight practice correctly. As a result, most insight exercises usually include a focus such as the breath to anchor the awareness in the present (for this reason, a light absorption state can be a great aid in practicing insight); however, whereas in concentration exercises all other sensations are excluded from awareness, in insight practice all experience is apprehended and allowed to arise and pass of its own accord in conjunction with the primary focus. It can be seen then that the difference between absorption and insight is a subtle one, and it is possible to initiate the stages of insight by any of the exercises used to attain absorption states by simply expanding, rather than contracting, the awareness during the practice. Classic examples of insight practice are vipassana, centred prayer, puja and other devotional practices, and gaining the Knowledge and Conversation of the Holy Guardian Angel (see chapter 13).

The metaphysical process is cyclical in nature and is composed of three basic stages: a plateau, a trough and a peak.

The plateau is a period of novelty, where magical practice is interesting and progress is steady. Insights come easily, and the plateau culminates in an event I like to call Naïve Enlightenment. Naïve enlightenment can include, but is not limited to, the following phenomena: trance-like events, dissolution of boundaries, visions of bright light, feelings of bliss, oneness, vibration, love, great enthusiasm for non-dualism, the belief you've experienced God/the Tao/the Truth, the belief enlightenment has occurred as a single event, as opposed to a process.

The trough quickly follows naïve enlightenment, and practice becomes difficult and unpleasant. The success enjoyed during the plateau is gone, and the magician can experience any number of negative emotions, at varying degrees of intensity, in regard to perception itself. The trough can include, but is not limited to, the following phenomena: feelings of fear, disgust, and hate, desire for deliverance, psychosis, unpleasant bodily sensations, and sleepiness. The trough is sometimes referred to in other systems as the 'Dark Night of the Soul', and can last anywhere from a few hours to a number of years, the latter usually as a result of buying into the naïve enlightenment event.

The peak arrives with a gradual equanimity towards phenomena: peace is made with perception. Magick is no longer the slog it was during the trough, and a certain feeling of mastery prevails. The peak reaches a climax with the occurrence of the absolute as a peak experience. This marks a fundamental insight into the nature of reality, and with repetition of the cycle the occurrence of the absolute will develop into a plateau experience, with the eventual end result of the process being complete illumination or enlightenment with the occurrence of the absolute as a permanent adaptation.

For a more in-depth discussion of the metaphysical process, please see my essay *Crossing the Abyss: How to do it and what to expect.*

It should be noted that many teachers and traditions in both the East and West have confused absorption states with insight stages, with some practitioners being completely oblivious to the fact that a metaphysical process with stages even exists at all. Considering the ease in which an absorption state practice can become an insight exercise, it should come as no surprise that many dabblers in magical techniques have accidentally initiated the process only to become effectively 'stuck' in a stage without realising it, let alone knowing how to progress. This can spell bad news if the stage happens to be the trough! The only remedy to such a situation is the habitual practice of insight. If that doesn't sound too appealing, or if you would rather not engage with the process, it is best not to dabble with magick at all.

In the end, the difference between a state and a stage is a question of immediate access: if a mystical event can be experienced at will, and the access and intensity of that experience can be improved with repetition, we are most certainly looking at a state that we can enter and exit. If a mystical event occurs, but can only be repeated after passing through a number of recognisable events beforehand, we are looking at a stage of the metaphysical process.

EXERCISE 22

1. Sit comfortably, preferably in a meditation posture.

2. Select an object to concentrate on. This can be anything from a spot on the wall, a sound or mantra or a visualized shape such as a yellow square.

3. Fix your attention on the object. Every time you become aware of something other than the object, simply return your attention to it. This will occur frequently at first, but will improve with time.

4. Persist for at least 15 minutes in the beginning, extending the sitting period as your ability develops.

5. Record any results including the number of breaks from the object.

6.   In addition to the above exercise, study and experiment with as many trance inducing practices as possible, and record the results.

EXERCISE 23

Compare and contrast the results from exercise 22, above, with the exercises given in Chapters 12 and 14.

NON-DUAL

The ultimate level of experience is a mystery. Experience of the non-dual is not really an experience at all, as by its very nature no 'experiencer' or experience is possible at this level, but nevertheless the practices that engage the metaphysical stages of insight lead to the occurrence of the non-dual during the peak of the cycle. Repetition of the insight cycle will eventually lead to the occurrence of the non-dual as a permanent adaptation, which is when the magician is considered illuminated or enlightened. This is the Great Work of magick.

Whereas every other level of experience demonstrates relative and subjective shallow features as well as objective deep features, the non-dual is the only level that is absolute and objective *in itself*. The non-dual is the truth with a capital T.

Reality

Although I've categorised experience as physical, etheric, emotional, mental, astral, metaphysical and non-dual, it must be borne in mind that we never experience these various levels in isolation. Reality is the total experience of all these levels simultaneously—even when focused on one particular experience we are still experiencing every other level, even if we aren't immediately aware of the fact. The totality of reality is therefore our available means of manifestation, and so the greater our mastery of each of the levels of experience, the greater the variety and depth of the magical results we can enjoy.

Magick, when practiced at all levels, is the expansion of the self in all directions.

10. The Dirty F-Word

Or:

'An Introduction To Working With Spirits, Gods And Demons'

One of the most rewarding fields of magical practice is interaction with non-human intelligences, or working with spirits and gods. This can take many forms, from creating your own entities to practicing a religion.

In the monotheistic mainstream traditions of the West, faith is the means by which we interact with non-human intelligences. For many magicians, faith has become synonymous with swallowing authoritarian dogma via a complete circumvention of the reasoning faculty, and as such is now considered a bit of a dirty word.

Anyone For Cake?

So what is the difference between magical interaction with spirits and the Western monotheistic traditions, or what we usually call religion? What immediately springs to mind is ineffectual ritual.

From the age of three, up until I was ten, I sang hymns and prayed daily at a Church of England school. In that seven-year period, nothing spiritual in terms of the Christian narrative ever happened to me. I never saw evidence of God, Jesus or Mary; I never had a prayer answered; I never felt 'a presence'. That cardboard had no meaty goodness.

There is of course the question of sincerity. Did God ignore me because I lacked faith? There are Christians who claim experience of their God—and the glassy look in their eyes as they smugly hug themselves is enough to convince me of genuine experience. Yet I distinctly remember believing in Jesus and his gaseous dad; after all, they got me at a young age. So the fault must lie in what I was actually *doing*.

SILLY BOB

Let us consider prayer. In the Church of England, this generally involves heaping praise on God, expounding your inadequacies as a worthless wretch, and then asking for forgiveness. It's pretty obvious you're not exactly commanding Big G into a 'triangle of art'. And when you get specific, kneeling at your bed, asking 'Please Lord, help Bob 'No Knees' Robson see the error of his gambling ways, etc', you are hoping, desiring, that God will respond. However, your desire is the qualification of the absence of what you actually want—i.e. you are experiencing this event: *I hope a god will listen to me*.

If we look at magical practice or religious traditions where spirits or gods can be traded with, or compelled, we can see that the interaction is the qualification of the requested result. The experience here is: *I am interacting with a god*. Appropriate results must necessarily follow.

Those Christians that have experienced their God *must have decided to*.

What you experience in terms of your interaction with non-human intelligences rests in a magical decision. As such, we must question what we mean when we use the word 'faith'. I began this chapter with the common definition of faith as being that of 'an unquestioning belief in something, regardless of proof'.

I offer a re-evaluation: 'Faith' is at the heart of every single experience you have, because what you experience rests solely on a *decision*, which does not require an explanation for it to exist.

Faith is such a dirty word for non-religious Westerners because our primary example is a decision to have no result; therefore, we think faith means blind belief with no apparent benefit. In terms of Christianity, faith is simply the decision to have no experience of God. When we practice magick with a spirit, even in the absence of any physical indication of its presence, our faith is the decision to interact with that entity.

DEATH = HAPPY TIME

So why on earth would a Christian/Jew/Muslim choose to have no experience of his or her God?

Well, there is a certain amount of coercion from the governing bodies: as long as we remain in a state of desire when we petition God, we won't face eternal damnation in the afterlife.

If we look at the monotheistic system as a whole, we can see that it is based on keeping the devotee in a state of desire *permanently*. It is not your place to demand anything from God, so you must hope; the benefit of devotion is promised at the end of your earthly existence, so you must remain in a state of desire. And let us not forget, bonking is very bad.

Desire is a magical act that leads nowhere. Desire is a prison.

Any other magical act necessitates a move away from desire, and is therefore a move towards freedom.

Time To Get The Tin-Foil Hats Out

The Church has been very sneaky, using magick to render its members *permanently ineffectual*, whilst denying or damning the very thing that keeps them in that state. Which begs the question—did the creators of these religions (and by this I don't mean Christ, Moses or Mohammed) know what they were doing?

At this point, it would be very easy for me to make the claim that there is an ancient, secret global network of black magicians, which aeons ago created organised monotheistic religion in order to enslave mankind for its own dark ends.

But then, I don't want to get kicked out, do I?

11. GOD BOTHERING

OR:
'HOW TO WORK WITH SPIRITS, GODS AND DEMONS'

Working with spirits, gods or other entities is very simple: *you decide to*. Like this:

1. Decide why you want to work with an entity (this can be anything, from a specific reason like wanting to increase your wealth, to the exercise of religious devotion).

2. Pick an appropriate entity (so if you wanted to perform some magick related to love, an appropriate goddess to work with might be Venus. There is also no reason you can't pick the spirit of someone who has died to work with, like an ancestor[8]).

---

8. If you choose an entity that would love to ruin your life and your mental well being, make sure you work with it in the traditional method, or with some other form of protection. As an example, there is a group of spirits known as the Goetia (to be found in *The Lesser Key of Solomon the King*) that traditionally require various names of God, a triangle for the spirit to be conjured into, and a circle for the magician to stand in, for the protection of the magician. I have encountered numerous ma-

3. Choose a representation of the entity to work with; this could be physical (like a painting or statue—either bought or made by yourself), or imagined (by visualising the entity's form— what does it look like/smell like/sound like?).

Alternatively, if you know it, you can just work with the entity's sigil or seal in place of the entity's actual form.

Remember: if you choose to visualise the entity, it doesn't mean you are not addressing a real intelligence; what you experience is the truth.

4. Now talk to him or her. If you don't know what to say, consider how you would talk to any stranger. Be polite and friendly.

5. If you know what the entity likes, give him or her an offering, and in return ask for help with whatever problem may be at hand. It feels silly to have to say this, but remember: if you want to interact with the entity, you must decide to interact with the entity, by doing it.

---

gicians who think such protection is superfluous, their argument usually being 'other cultures don't need protection to interact with their spirits.' But that's because their spirits aren't the Goetia. It is true that many African/Caribbean/Brazilian traditions (such as Quimbanda or Voudon) interact with spirits that share similar names and seals with Goetic spirits, but these spirits are still not the Goetia. If you want to work with the Goetia, then work with the whole of the Goetia. If you work with the Goetic demons without protection, they will fuck you up. Badly. If you want to work with spirits the way 'other traditions' do, without protection, then work with spirits that do not require it.

Offerings can take many forms, such as food, flowers, alcohol, tobacco, art works and even breath. Two of the most 'powerful' offerings that entities from all walks of life seem to prize above all others, are blood and sex.

Offering blood does not require amputation or murder (disappointing, I know)—a single drop of blood extracted via a sterilised lancet and dabbed on the entities representation will suffice.

Similarly, in the case of a sexual sacrifice, an orgy isn't necessary (but if you're going to be at one anyway, what the hell?). Simply anointing the entity with sexual fluids from a dedicated act of masturbation is adequate.

It must be stressed that both blood and sex sacrifices should only be used in extreme cases—they guarantee exceptional results, but if used frequently some spirits will expect *nothing less* in the future—and then where do you go from there?

6. Once you've said everything you need to say, thank the entity and say goodbye.

7. It is customary to perform a banishing ritual here—see below for details.

HELLO? IS ANYBODY THERE?

It must be remembered that non-human intelligences can only communicate through what is available—if you don't have great visionary ability, don't expect the entity to pop up and shake your hand.

If all you do is address the entity, give an offering, ask for help and give thanks, without any visible manifestation or a booming voice or objects floating around your room, *the magick will still work* (unless, of course, you're rude and expect something for nothing).

If you want more than a one-way conversation, it can be prudent to offer a means of communication when working with a spirit, such as a divinatory device like a pendulum or Ouija board. Another good means is to ask the entity to communicate with you through your dreams.

Unless an entity has a special interest in you (this does happen), it may take a while before the entity starts visiting you spontaneously or helping you out at times of need without being asked. This is when the real benefit of forming a relationship with a non-human intelligence becomes apparent.

Now The Ritual Is Over, What Do I Do With The Body?

On a practical note, if you've decided to give your entity an offering that isn't actually used up during the ritual (such as incense), what do you actually do with it after the ritual?

Well, short of the entity actually telling you what to do with it, I would recommend leaving food offerings on the altar, or in some other place it would not be disturbed, until it starts to smell. I would then either bury it somewhere, rededicating to the entity, or if the offering has been there for some time, throw it away. In the case of something that already smells, such as a bleeding cow's heart, the faster it gets in the ground, the better.

In the case of alcohol or other drinks, you could leave them to evaporate, or pour them, rededicated, as a libation on the earth.

Objects, such as works of art, can be buried or burned.

Saying that though, there's nothing quite like a big pile of cigars, flowers, burning incense, candles, bizarre fetishes and numerous bottles of 40% rum to make your altar look the business[9].

HOW TO CREATE FAMILIARS

Of course, you don't have to work with an existing god or spirit. You can always make one up. This type of spirit is usually referred to as a familiar or servitor. If you can think of a task you would like a spirit to do, consider what kind of spirit might be most appropriate for the job. What would it look like? Sound like? Smell like? Give it a name and/or a sigil. Next, visualise it, address it and ask it to perform the task. Alternatively, you can find/make a material representation of the spirit, and address that.

Remember to be specific and don't expect the spirit to come running back with a big bag of gold if you've asked it to get you some cash—the result will manifest as a synchronicity.

---

9. A word of warning: if you, or an ignorant friend, decide to take a dedicated offering off of the altar for yourself, then you are stealing from a spirit. I shall say no more.

Prolonged use of the spirit will strengthen it—if you visualise the familiar's form, it will progressively become more vivid and may appear when you don't call it—becoming more adept at its job to boot.

HOW TO DO A BANISHING

So what do you do when your created entity starts getting on your tits (for example, throwing crap around your gaff)? Well, it's probably time to get rid of it. In terms of a created familiar, you could visualise the spirit dissolving into energy that you reabsorb, or you could burn its material representation and sigil. To get rid of an entity you have summoned, you will require a banishing ritual.

Many people believe that banishing serves no other function than psychological reassurance. But as I have said, if you decide that's what it does, then that's what it does. Personally, I prefer to throw uninvited demons (that jump on me in the middle of the night) out of my house, rather than just fostering a feeling of being 'centred'.

I find it's generally a good idea to banish before any magical act in order to remove any lurking 'influences' afterwards (unless of course you want whatever it is you have summoned to linger around).

Banishing, like all acts of magick, can take any number of forms, the limit of which is your imagination. For example, if you have any friends that happen to be a god or spirit, you can ask these to aid you in banishing the space, or alternatively you can command any unwanted influences to disperse in the name of a god or spirit. You can even visualise a vacuum cleaner sucking up any lingering thoughts and feelings, or a bright light that dissolves any unwanted presences (perhaps growing out of your head to encompass the space).

Of course, there are many traditional forms of exorcism or banishing available, such as the *Lesser Banishing Ritual of the Pentagram*, the *Gnostic Pentagram Banishing Ritual*, and the *Star Ruby*, should you want somewhere to start.

How To Get Possessed

Possession, invocation or channelling—whatever you want to call it, letting an entity communicate through your body is good fun.

There are two very simple traditional methods for achieving this:

1. Address the entity in exactly the same way as described previously, and ask or call it to possess you (or, if you are working in a group, then ask or call the spirit to possess the chosen 'horse'—this is the person to be possessed, whom the entity will 'ride').

2. Pretend to be the entity, adopting its form through an act of imagination, and through speaking as though you *are* the entity, until the entity starts acting through you with no conscious effort on your behalf.

However, from what we know of the magical act, it is possible to get possessed by an entity through other means, from the sympathetic method to a completely nonsensical act. For instance, you could tap a picture of yourself with a statue of the chosen entity, until you are possessed, or you could decide that you will be possessed by *n* (insert chosen entity name) through eating some 'charged' bread, and awaiting the result.

The duration of the magical act used for the spirit to possess you, before you get the desired result, will vary from ritual to ritual, and from 'horse' to 'horse'. It may be two minutes or it could be ten—just don't expect to suddenly black out and wake up an hour later, with mysterious bruises and someone else's trousers on.

Possession is a gradual process *and you need to let it happen* or you will dispel the effect.

Like all things, invocation may take a few attempts before you have any degree of real success; but it is a lot easier and a lot less frightening than the beginner might assume. It takes talent in this field or a good deal of practice before you can get to the stage of actually failing to recall what you did whilst you were possessed.

So what do you do once the entity has arrived?

Like any magical act, you should have a reason for doing it, and hopefully you've picked an entity that can help you with this.

Interact with the entity as described earlier—have a chat, make offerings, ask for oracular information or for help with a problem.

You may find that the possession will end of its own accord, and may not last as long as desired; either way, thank the entity for coming, say good-bye and banish.

In the case of a possession that lasts longer than desired, you will need to thank the entity, ask it to leave and banish, banish, banish! If in a group setting, administer a direct banishing on the individual (drawing a pentagram over the person is always a good one). In extreme cases, a bucket of cold water in the face has proven effective.

How To Conjure An Entity To Visible Manifestation

Come on, admit it—this is what you've been waiting for, isn't it?

Traditionally, the method is exactly the same as described at the beginning of this chapter (except you only work with a physical representation or sigil of the entity, not the visualisation of its form), but when you address the entity you ask or call it to visibly manifest, for as long as it takes to get a result, before you proceed with the rest of the ritual.

Again, as with invocation, you can get an entity to manifest using any experience you choose, just so long as you decide that it means that specific entity will manifest. For instance, you could have a magick Ganesha hat that whenever worn calls Ganesha to appear. Such an act would require repetition until any efficacy is developed—in just the same way as calling Ganesha to manifest in the traditional manner does.

The quality of the manifestation depends on a number of factors: the entity used, the experience of the conjurer (i.e. how much practice he or she has put in), but most importantly, the available means the entity has to manifest.

If you have a good visionary ability, then the greater the chance the entity has of visibly appearing *to you*. If not, you could burn a good quantity of incense for the entity to form a physical shape out of the smoke, or perhaps use a shiny surface (such as a black mirror with two candles at each side of it) to 'see' the entity in.

If you don't have much of a visionary faculty, and provide no other means, chances are you will have the unmistakable feeling of a presence, or perhaps a drop in temperature, as confirmation of manifestation. If you're lucky, the entity might even re-arrange the contents of your house for you.

Remember: you don't need to conjure the entity to manifest in order to work with it.

Now we've covered the various methods of working with entities, over the next page I've provided an example of a ritual using these methods, and how they correspond to the outline given in chapter 4.

Here we go again:

Exercise 24

1. Use each of the first four methods given in the table over the page, using a different entity

with each one, and employ the fifth method before and after each working.

2. Record the results.

EXERCISE 25

1. Choose one of the entities that you've already used.

2. Using your imagination, come up with some nonsensical action or experience (i.e. with no logical correspondence to the entity chosen or the act of manifestation).

3. Decide that this experience means your chosen entity will appear.

4. Practice, and record the results.

Outline	Entity work	Creating a familiar
1. Decide what you want to occur.	My manager will resign	I will create a familiar
2. Ensure that what you want to occur has a means of manifestation.	I do have a manager and there is the possibility for him to resign.	I have the faculty of visualisation
3. Choose an experience.	The addressing of a fetish of the Aztec god Tezcatlipoca, with an offering of chocolate.	The visualisation and addressing of a little elf
4. Decide that the experience means the same thing as what you want to occur.	Giving an offering to Tezcatlipoca to ensure my manager resigns means my manager will resign	The visualisation of a little elf means I will create a familiar
5. Perform the act/ undergo the experience.	Address Tezcatlipoca, ask him to help make your manager resign, thank him and give him the chocolate. Banish. Later on, bury the offering.	Visualise a little elf, give it a name, and tell him he will appear whenever you call, to carry out whatever tasks you wish him to perform
6. Result.	Within a day / week / month?	Whenever you need a bit of magick doing, call the familiar's name (it might take a few goes before he appears without needing to be visualised) and instruct him

Traditional possession method	Traditional visible manifestation method	Banishing
I will be possessed by n.	I will conjure n to visible manifestation	I will banish any entities present
The entity can manifest through my body	The entity can manifest using the smoke from the copious amounts of incense I will burn	Entities can stop manifesting
Imagining myself as n, and describing my attributes as n.	The calling of n to visibly appear.	Drawing 4 pentagrams in the air with my finger, one at each compass point (N,E,S,W).
By imagining myself as n I will become possessed by n	By calling n to visibly appear I will conjure n to visible manifestation	By drawing 4 pentagrams in the cardinal directions I will banish any entities present
Imagine yourself as n, describe yourself as n and your attributes as n.	Call n to visibly appear.	Draw 4 pentagrams, one at each of the cardinal points.
Result manifests at the end of step 5.	Result manifests at the end of step 5 (how this manifests depends on what the entity has available to work with)	Result manifests at the end of step 5.

12. One Portion Of Death, Please

'The Nature Of Initiation'

Stereotypically, the occult scene is rife with lamenting traditionalists, decrying the lack of respect epitomised in the 'cherry-picking' activities of the chaos magician. The chaos magician, on the other hand, proclaims with a postmodern sneer: I am free from the traditionalists' ignorance! Why not have magick without the dogma?

Sadly, some stereotypes are true, and you don't need to look far on the occult scene to see these particular examples in action. Magick, it seems, is as infected by prejudice[10] as any other culture.

However I believe this bickering and posturing is indicative of a genuine problem with both approaches; and this is no better illustrated than in the magicians that feel the need to either convert from one stance to the other, or to keep a foot in both camps. True enough, some conversions are simply a case of changing stripes and maintaining

---

10. As disgusting as it is, I've actually experienced the wrong end of these prejudices in action.

the same childish behaviour; but there are a number for whom the need is genuine.

Why is this? What is missing from the postmodern approach for its adherents to yearn for a transition or a complimentary commitment to a single tradition?

HAND OVER THE SECRET FORMULA

One of the biggest criticisms of postmodern magick concerns its lack of initiatory knowledge. Traditions have teachings that cannot be learned from books, but must be transmitted orally, or demonstrated. Without initiation into the tradition, these techniques or secrets cannot be known. With regards to postmodern magick, even membership to a practical magical order will only confer a certain level of practical prowess, with the practitioner remaining on his or her own with regards to anything outside the realm of suggested practical methodology—which is generally available in any good bookshop. The postmodern approach will not tell you 'the truth', or provide you with meaning, nor address any moral or cultural implications in the use of magick. Is the chaos magician missing out on something here? Does the traditionalist really have something the rest of the occult scene doesn't know about, perhaps a secret technique beyond anything we can order over the internet?

When it comes to the postmodern practical methodology, you are given free reign to use any technique from any tradition, which can easily induce option anxiety—with so much to choose from, how do you know where to start?

This can be a big stumbling block for beginners and adepts alike. The inability to know where you are going can be wearing after a prolonged period. The problem is compounded by the fact that some postmodern magicians will even stress that anything outside of a material result *is not magick*. The developmental maps of the Qabalists, Gnostics, Alchemists, Sufis, Buddhists, Hindus and Hermeticists are deconstructed and discarded as either primitive cosmologies or hopelessly antiquarian moralities.

Indeed, we are told that 'nothing is true, everything is permitted'. If we regard all ideas as relative, and so of equal or no intrinsic value, how can we fail to see the search for truth as inherently pointless? It doesn't take much to come to the conclusion that not only magick, but also existence itself, is meaningless.

Faced with that, it isn't hard to see the attraction of a magical tradition, however dogmatic.

Goggles

The trouble is, the distinction between practicality and the provision of truth is a false one.

The idea that you can be taught meaning through ideas is like believing you can swim because you've read a book about it.

Any degree of practical success with magick is indicative that you are on the right track. Everything to be learnt *about* magick can be garnered from the actual experience itself. It only takes a little experience before it is apparent that magick is too simple, and so too big a phenomenon, to be kept as any kind of secret by any tradition.

Now, whether you gain this experience within a single complete cosmogony, handed down through generations, or you investigate possible narratives that might explain what you have experienced *after the fact*, is of absolutely no consequence. There is no intrinsic value in explanation, beyond its use in the magical act.

Both traditionalism and postmodernism (despite appearances) offer *the* truth. Traditionalism swears by its 'teachings', whilst postmodernism declares 'all truth is relative'.

Both fail to realise that the truth is *experience*, not the words used to describe that experience. The traditionalist fails to understand the arbitrary nature of any idea, whereas the postmodernist fails to understand that the truth is not in the relativity of those ideas, but in experience itself.

If we recognise the magical act as a means of *experiencing* truth (as opposed to offering *the* truth), with necessary artistic, scientific and cultural aspects, then affiliation to a magical approach, whether postmodern or traditional, ceases to be a matter of finding *the one correct answer* and becomes a matter of aesthetic, cultural or transformational relevance. Do you like dressing up as a witch and raising cones of power in the woods? Or do chaospheres get you all hot under the collar? Do you want to be bossed around by an egomaniac, knowing that one day you'll discover the secrets of the universe, or would you rather create your own cult?

The recognition of truth as a revelatory experience is to live in a world of boundless meaning, free from dogma. We understand the world, yet that understanding is continually overthrown by a richer, deeper and greater comprehension. Existence is transformed from a word into an experience.

Ultimately, the *experience* of practicing magick, not the people you practice it with, or the methods or ideas you use, is the only guru you will ever need.

Apple For The Teacher

It is customary in all magical approaches, traditional or otherwise, for the aspirant to undergo initiation. The word itself can be traced to ancient Greece where one of its many meanings was death. Initiation usually involves undergoing some kind of ordeal in a ritual setting, sometimes with a death / rebirth element, that marks a definite step away from what you were, and a step towards what you want to be.

In magical terms, you cease to be an ordinary human and become a magician.

The benefits of undergoing initiation are numerous. As stated earlier, in magical tradition this will usually involve access to previously hidden techniques or 'secrets' that the teacher or guru will hand down to the initiate, and more often than not functions as a formal recognition of some kind of attainment. It is not necessary to belong to an occult body in order to be initiated; however it can be beneficial to undergo an initiation ritual regardless of whether or not you do. This can be as simple or as complex as you like, and it is probably a good idea to incorporate a symbolic discarding of old, outmoded habits or ways of being, and an acceptance of new characteristics you wish to have.

Initiation can best be summed up as *a transformation of the self*.

Ring Any Bells?

You can consider this an initiation if you like, because I'm going to let you in on a little secret. Although many magicians place a lot of value in undergoing ritual initiations (especially the ones that like to feel 'special'), if initiation is transformation, then you underwent initiation the moment you performed your first magical act.

Furthermore, every revelatory or transformative experience, from the moment you first used your lungs to the reading of this sentence, must be part of an initiatory process. As an exercise in revelation, the practice of magick can be considered an acceleration of this process. However, due to the very nature of revelation, *initiation never ends*.

Whether or not you are practicing a single tradition, or maintaining a postmodern approach, whether you practice alone or in a group, whether you are reading this because you have a genuine interest in magick or you just fancied a laugh, you are already part of an initiatory process. Secrets and privileges are for the deluded.

Of course, initiation that is predominantly concerned with one level of experience, such as the physical, does not necessitate a transformation at every other level, such as the emotional or intellectual. For instance, it is possible to undergo the initiations of puberty and middle age without ever engaging with the metaphysical process, or to develop rapidly at the etheric level whilst remaining completely ignorant of the astral.

Initiation never ends, but it progresses at wildly different rates with each individual and at each level.

Green Mist

Although everyone is part of an initiatory process, it doesn't mean that everyone is a magician, or that every magician is good at magick. You need not be a magician to experience transformation, and if you are a magician, your magical ability rests on a level of development that is dependent on magical practice; so although many people may seem light years ahead of you in terms of obtaining magical results, your ability is not limited by any idea of natural talent or genetics. Rather, it simply means the more successful magicians have a greater experience of initiation, which is something you can remedy by implementing a regime of daily magical practice.

CONVEYOR BELT

At first glance it may appear curious that the end result of the metaphysical process, or experience of the non-dual level of experience, is considered the prime focus of practicing magick by all genuine magical traditions, as illustrated in magical developmental maps such as the Qabalists' Tree of Life, the alchemical process, or the various stages of insight found in Theravada Buddhism. The goal is usually referred to as 'enlightenment', or as it is known in the West, 'The Great Work'.

But didn't I just state initiation never ends?

Although the practice of magick is the expansion of the self in all directions and at all levels of experience, the non-dual is unique in that it transcends but includes all other levels. In other words, although initiation never ends as a peculiar expression at each level of experience, the direction of that initiation is ultimately and inescapably towards the non-dual. As the only true objective and absolute level of experience, the non-dual is not part of the process itself (every other level of experience) and so is the only genuine accomplishment possible.

The Great Work can only be accomplished *because* initiation never ends.

WAIT A MINUTE...

But if revelation cannot be known before it has happened, how can we possibly name, describe and predict a number of 'revelatory' states or the goal of the Great Work to form a developmental map?

The problem lies with thinking revelation cannot be known; rather, revelation is *experienced*. Any idea of knowing or not knowing is simply not applicable. Although a map might provide the layout of the streets and an expectation of what can be found in a town, it is not the experience of visiting that town. In the same fashion, we can chart our progress and catch our 'initiatory' bearings from the maps drawn by previous magicians, but the words or diagrams are not the transformative, revelatory experience itself.

The value in any map is in how well it describes and predicts your experience; whether you come to it through an actual decision to work within that map, *à la* belief shifting, is of no consequence. Without corroborating experience, the map is nothing more than a superfluous explanation.

A Means Of Revelatory Manifestation

If we were to consider an exclusive magical act for revelatory experience at the metaphysical level, it might look something like the table over the page.

Outline	Revelatory magical act
1. Decide what you want to oc-cur.	I will experience revelation/enlightenment (or whatever the goal of a particular magic-al model may be).
2 Ensure that what you want to occur has a means of mani-festation.	We require revelatory experience at the profound or metaphysical level of experi-ence—so the means of manifestation is you. Perhaps addressing this level would therefore provide a better means of mani-festation.
3. Choose an ex-perience.	In the light of point 2, an experience could be anything from a simple posture, which could include hand gestures, movements, mantra or visualisation, all the way up to a full-blown ritual act (see chapter 14 for an example of this).
4. Decide that the experience means the same thing as what you want to occur.	Let's say you've decided to sit in a certain posture for number 3.
5. Perform the act/undergo the experience.	Sit, and experience sitting. This means maintaining awareness of the present ex-perience, without making the experience about something else, for a given period of time (for example 15 minutes).
6. Result.	What this result may be depends solely on 'where' you are in terms of magical/initiat-ory development at the metaphysical level (the available means of manifestation). This is where predictive magical models or maps become indispensable.

This magical act is usually referred to as Zazen, or sitting meditation in Zen Buddhism, and it is one of the simplest and most direct methods of experiencing profound revelation or the metaphysical stages of insight.

No doubt you may well object, especially if you've actually tried meditation, that one act of sitting in a posture does not lead to 'enlightenment'. This is correct, and you can be forgiven for thinking that the above ritual outline suggests that this is so.

However, revelation at the metaphysical level is not a single event, state or experience, but a continuous process, as outlined in chapter 9. This process is inseparable from the means of manifestation.

To perform an act of magick for the end goal of a magical developmental model, and expect a result that does not include the process it describes, is akin to performing a ritual for money without figuring the physical or 'real' world into the result, and expecting hard cash to materialise out of thin air. Again, magick does not allow you to do anything outside of that which exists.

EXERCISE 26

1. Investigate as many esoteric developmental models and meditative practices as possible, such as those found in Alchemy, Qabalah,

Yoga, Buddhism, Sufism, Taoism, Hermeticism, Gnosticism, Thelema, Tantra, etc[11].

2. Practice magick everyday, including some form of insight meditation, such as Zazen as outlined above. Here's another example called vipassana:

- Sit comfortably.
- Rest the attention on the physical sensations that constitute the body.
- Do not try and exclude any other sensations—such as persistent thoughts or feelings—just allow them to arise and pass of their own accord.
- Begin by sitting for 15 minutes at a time, increasing the duration as you progress.
- When you forget what you are supposed to be doing, simply bring the attention back to the body.

If you need a structure for your daily magical practice, you can either devise one based on the exercises given in this book, or you can choose an existing set of techniques from the plethora of magical approaches, such as the eight limbs of yoga, *Liber KKK* as given in *Liber Kaos* by Peter Carroll, the Invocation of the Holy Guardian Angel (see chapter 14 for details), Taoist energy work, etc.

Remember: you can practice as many techniques, both original and traditional, side by side

---

11. Please see the suggested reading list given at the end of this book.

for as long or as short a period of time as you see fit. Just make sure you do something everyday!

3. Continually monitor the results obtained and the applicability of the various developmental maps to your experience, regardless of whether you have taken your daily practice from a specific model or not.

13. Making Omelettes

Or:

The Prophetic Narrative

It is pretty obvious, especially once you get over the shock that it actually works, that magick demonstrates something about the nature of reality that is incredibly difficult to explain. However, this doesn't stop people from trying, especially in the West where we are obsessed with finding 'The One Correct Answer'.

Gandalf The Master Wizard

I once had the good fortune of participating in a group magical working (if you haven't tried this yet, it's really easy—get a group of friends together, and bring a ritual each for the whole group to perform). In the aftermath of a ritual to destroy our consensual reality via the detonation of an ontological grenade, all three participants experienced the same thought, literally. This is a phenomenon otherwise known as telepathy—in our minds at least, the rite had worked.

However, the aftermath of the ritual happened to involve the beginning of another ritual, with the aim of constructing or contacting the group egregore. A group egregore can be considered the sum of the members' personalities, and therefore an additional member of the group. As we began the process of building the egregore's personality, we experienced one of the egregore's characteristics *as a group thought*. It was pretty obvious that we were in direct contact with the group spirit. The rite was off to a flying start (the poltergeist activity later on proved the rite a definite success, although that's another story).

So, which working was responsible for the telepathy? Did the grenade rite seem effectual only because it preceded the effect of the egregore ritual? Or was the grenade responsible for the telepathy, and it just seemed as though we experienced egregore contact due to the context of the group-mind ritual?

Gandalf The Masturbator

There is of course a third option: there was no telepathy, because telepathy doesn't exist; there occurred a coincidence of similar thoughts, which just so happened during a demented bout of non-sensical, naïve buffoonery in an incense-clogged room.

It would be customary here to debate which view should be considered 'the truth'. If there were a bunch of magicians discussing this with a materialist, the magical view would win outright as the consensual view; and vice versa: one magician against a board of paranormal debunkers would only inform a non-magical reality.

However, if we look at debate as the function of assimilating experience into a person's model of reality, or narrative, I think it would be more prudent to investigate the question itself: what really happened?

Lord God, Why?

Why must we insist on *one* event occurring? It seems to me that this insistence is based on the idea of a false choice-restriction: you can have either/or, but not also/and. And what's with the insistence of determining a 'true' cause? Again, we are back to the either/or option.

It's pretty obvious that all three viewpoints fit the bill, so why pick one over the other? If not for aesthetic reasons, if not for the most optimistic, intoxicating or empowering experience a view will afford, then what is there?

Does anyone really prefer to be a meat robot, trapped on a rock floating in the infinite cold, in an unforgiving, pointless universe that happened by chance? Alone, insignificant, with only two weeks on a beach each year to look forward to?

If we entertain the idea of also/and, we can have two successful rites that demonstrate a mind-blowing, fun and genuinely exciting existence, the consequence of which is a further exploration of superhuman powers and the development of a relationship with a non-human intelligence. Or you can go to Tenerife.

TOOL

Now the sharpest amongst you may have spotted a problem with the idea of accepting more than one viewpoint—and that is the common occult behaviour of *arbitrary cause assignment*. To practice magick for a desired result is an exercise in causality—you are attempting to cause an event, and should your magick work, you take the credit as the cause of the event's manifestation.

Any magician worth his or her salt will tell you that your desire will manifest as a synchronicity; everyday events appear to lead to your result. The idea that the event is a coincidence becomes a moot point when for the one-hundredth rite you get your one-hundredth coincidence. To lay the cause of the event at the feet of the chaos of the normal world is symptomatic of a person unable to assimilate the story of magick into their narrative.

However, what happens when the event doesn't materialise? Or, better yet, what happens when you get a series of events that all overlap (like the example with which I began this chapter)? We rapidly approach a situation of convenient 'cause' assignment, which engenders that ancient mystical phenomenon: *talking crap*.

ERM, IT WAS LIKE THAT WHEN I GOT HERE

Immersion in magick and the results obtained by practice will repeatedly lead the practitioner to a causality impasse—i.e. the idea just does not fit the experience.

Now, you can carry on assigning 'cause' in a painfully obvious fashion, or you can fundamentally revise your narrative. No, I don't mean accepting Jesus into your heart—I'm talking about addressing the idea of cause and effect.

After a couple of years of daily practice, you may find something odd occurring: you begin manifesting results *without doing the actual work.* That's right—you think something, and it happens. Alas, this isn't as great as it sounds, as it tends to be those 'off-hand' or flippant thoughts that materialise; any conscious effort to control the ability tends to dispel it.

There is a real danger of becoming an armchair 'Secret Chief' when this happens, or falling into a state of paranoia about what events in your life you may be causing by accident.

For the sake of sanity, some magicians advocate ignoring this phenomenon and concentrating solely on tried and tested techniques when pursuing a result.

But to dismiss magical practice as unnecessary, or the phenomenon itself on the grounds you might go loopy, is a failure to realise *you have outgrown your narrative*.

If you are experiencing magical results without the magical practice, what does this say about *the practice itself*? If we look at what occurs in an existential sense, we do not actually experience a cause. We see two consecutive events that share the same meaning—i.e. a synchronicity. There is no difference here between a full-blown rite and a thought, other than a certain amount of effort. You are simply experiencing an increase in synchronicities, or to put it more precisely, your world has become more meaningful.

'But', cries the Secret Chief, 'if there is no cause, why would you perform a rite? What would be the point?'

Again, this is a failure to grasp that there is no difference between the thought and the rite; in practical terms, which necessitates operating in a causal narrative, *you carry on as you always have done.* The idea of something having a point (or being pointless) is simply not applicable when we 'step out' of causality.

No, I Said 'The Prophet Was Hammered'

A re-adjustment to a world based on synchronicity, as opposed to causality, is a step into the prophetic narrative.

At the beginning of a magician's career, synchronicity will occur as a *peak experience*. The magician performs a ritual in the temple, and later a real world event will occur sharing the same meaning. Causality is perfectly apt as a model for describing this experience.

With continued daily practice, synchronicities will begin to occur that are not strictly related to specific magical acts. Synchronicity becomes a *plat-*

eau experience, and the magician experiences periodic bouts of high weirdness. At this point it should become obvious that something far stranger than causality is required to account for this kind of magical experience.

Eventually, synchronicity will become a *permanent adaptation*. The advanced magician inhabits a world completely saturated with meaning, and the prophetic narrative has replaced causality as the magician's *modus operandi*.

Prophecy is often confused with prediction: the foretelling of a specific event. However, as described above, prophecy deals with synchronicity or the occurrence of events with the same meaning. If one event occurs, another (or more) will occur that shares a fundamentally similar nature. As such, the prophetic narrative is an attitude or viewpoint, and includes all magical effects, not simply the art of predicting the future, which is known as divination.

On The Cards

In order to divine an answer to a question, it is necessary to have a number of representations of possible answers to that question; and so the better divinatory systems, such as the I Ching and Tarot, have evolved into complete maps of reality where all phenomena can be attributed to a 'correct place' or meaning. The continued use of such maps will not only give you the ability to foresee the future i.e. the symbols you read for your answer will share the same nature as a future event, but will go some way to facilitating a move into the prophetic narrative, or of experiencing the world in terms of meaning.

Over the next page is a table that shows how a number of methods of divination fit within the context of the magical act. Have a look at the table, then come back and consider the following exercises:

EXERCISE 27

1. Investigate an existing method of divination that offers a complete map of the world, such as the Tarot or the I Ching.

2. Perform a reading for the day or week ahead for a period of a month or longer, and record the results.

EXERCISE 28

1. Investigate an existing method of divination that offers simple 'yes' and 'no' answers, such as the pendulum or ouija board.

2. Perform a divination for the day or week ahead for the period of a month or longer, and record the results.

EXERCISE 29

1. Invent your own method of divination.

2. Perform a divination for the day or week ahead for the period of a month or longer, and record the results.

It must be remembered that prophecy does not mean we have no freewill, or that everything is a matter of fate. Both of these ideas are simply *not applicable*, because we have removed the necessity of a cause, such as the self in terms of freewill, or the idea of God or destiny in the case of fate.

It does, however, mean that the cornerstone of existence is *meaning*.

Outline	Tarot
1. Decide what you want to occur.	I will receive an answer to my question.
2. Ensure that what you want to occur has a means of manifestation.	I have a complete map of existence made up of 72 symbols.
3. Choose an experience.	Shuffling the cards and laying them out in a certain pattern.
4. Decide that the experience means the same thing as what you want to occur.	Shuffling the cards and laying them out means I will get an answer to my question.
5. Perform the act/undergo the experience.	Shuffle the cards, produce a layout.
6. Result.	Occurred at the end of step 5—read the cards.

I Ching	Pendulum	Self-made divinat- ory system
I will receive an answer to my question.	I will receive an answer to my question.	I will receive an an- swer to my ques- tion.
I have a complete map of existence made up of 64 symbols.	I have a method of obtaining two an- swers, one for 'yes' and one for 'no'.	I have a self made map of the world or x amount of pos- sible answers.
Throwing sticks a number of times to build up a com- plete hexagram.	Letting the pendu- lum swing of its own accord.	Determined by my own ingenium.
Throwing the sticks will give me an answer to my question.	Letting the pendu- lum swing freely will give me an an- swer to my ques- tion.	Step 3 means the same as Step 1.
Throw the sticks, generate the hexa- gram	Let the pendulum hang freely, wait to see which way it swings.	Perform step 3.
Occurred at the end of step 5— read the hexa- gram.	Occurred at the end of step 5.	Occurred at the end of step 5.

ERM, WHAT DOES THAT MEAN?

It means that *explanation leads nowhere*. Causality is explanation—'this event is due to that event'. The proliferation of explanation has seen a world increasingly devoid of meaning. We know why things do the things they do. We can explain the functioning of the brain. We know how the universe can support life. But unless explanation is actually experienced, *it doesn't mean anything*.

Prophecy is not concerned with explanations or identification with specifics; events and even the symbols themselves (like 'you') are simply tokens. In the case of magick, the events that take place within the temple share the same nature as the events to which we would normally assign the idea of 'effect'. In other words, there is no difference between you (as part of the magical act) and the series of events you would normally call 'the result' (as both the magical act and the result, being a synchronicity, have the same meaning).

In other words, synchronicity is a dualistic expression of unity, and the more you experience meaning (the recognition of a number of events sharing the same nature) the more you become aware of the *experience itself* as opposed to any of the ideas we use to describe that experience.

Contrary to what many claim is an indulgence in escapism, magick is therefore a process of moving *into*, rather than away from, what is real; whereas explanation is to remove yourself from *what is actually happening now.*

Magick is the ecstatic embrace of life, and the resulting vision is prophecy.

14. Hover Boards And Silver Lycra

Or:

'The Greatest Act Of Magick That Can Be Performed'

If you were asked to describe what the greatest single act of magick is, what would you say? Depending upon how much experience you have, you might say evoking a demon to visible appearance, or the creation of a talisman to make yourself a sex god. What about a ritual to win the lottery?

Sure, they all sound good, but they're a bit transitory, and a wee bit materialistic. They're also the result of the current obfuscation of the Western Tradition.

What if, instead of a working to get one specific material result, we could perform a ritual that would give us the ability to achieve not just any material result we desired, but everything we've ever dreamed of—and furnish us with a complete understanding of the universe to boot?

I can't be sure if what I'm about to describe originated in the ancient African magical traditions, but it was certainly practiced in ancient Egypt[12], Hellenistic Greece and Europe over the last couple of centuries[13]. The greatest act of magick that can be performed is called the Invocation of the Holy Guardian Angel, or more recently, as the invocation of *the future magical self*. It is considered commensurate with performing the Great Work, and it is the Core Practice of the Western tradition of magick.

Everything else in this book, whether it is sigils, divination, evocation, possession, or meditation, is Support Practice and preparation for the Core Practice. Without this preparation, the means of manifestation for success in the Core Practice is severely limited. However, mastery of the Support Practices is not required as some transcendental magicians believe, and there is no need to spend years on end perfecting the various magical acts outlined in this book. Familiarity will suffice— once the lines are connected, the angel can speak, so why spend years polishing the phone before picking it up?

The Cheese Has Slid Off His Cracker

Whether we call it the Holy Guardian Angel (HGA) or the future magical self is of no consequence; it is simply a token representation that allows us to invoke (and so become) that which is completely beyond our current conception. If it helps, we can consider it a being with unlimited

---

12. See *The Sacred Magic of Abramelin the Mage.*
13. See Crowley's *Liber Samekh.*

magical power, unbound by space and time, and beyond life and death, but *no idea we have is big enough to describe it*. Hence, it is the embodiment of revelation at all levels, and so of magical power. *Ultimately, it is the non-dual itself.*

Although I will refer to this entity as your 'future magical self', it is completely independent from what you presently know as 'yourself'. It must be remembered that this being *is not you*. It is neither the best parts of yourself, nor how you would wish to be. Permanent identification with an over-blown idea (of yourself or anything else) will only send you stark raving bonkers. Remember: the HGA is not an idea, but the literal embodiment of that which is beyond conception.

As the nature of initiatory development is fundamentally revelatory, it is not possible to know at any given point upon the path what is necessary to advance (as we cannot know what the effects of a practice might be until we have been transformed by that practice, let alone where we are 'advancing' to), although we can make a pretty good guess. If we consider the HGA as the embodiment of that path (being your future magical self), and therefore the guru par excellence, once contact is made you find that what is necessary for the next transformation is 'presented' or 'brought to you' by your HGA (usually via synchronicity). No matter how beneficial the practices are that constitute a self-imposed regime, they are not informed by your future revelations and so can never yield the results that working with your HGA will bring. This doesn't mean that future work will not include the Support Practices performed prior to HGA contact; but it does mean that you will work less for greater results.

Like all magick, invoking your future magical self can be as simple or as complicated as you like. A good starting point is a banishing ritual (just so you don't get conned by a gnome pretending to be your HGA). However, it is imperative that you do not banish at the end of the working—after all, it is a process of transformation and so you want your future magical self to stick around.

In much the same way you would contact other entities, you can use/create/discover a sigil or representation of your future magical self, and then talk to him/her/it; invoke them, like this: 'I invoke you, my Holy Guardian Angel'. Again, asking your HGA to contact you via a dream has also proved useful, as have other divinatory tools such as a pendulum or tarot deck. It must be remembered though that it may take a lot of workings before actual manifestation occurs, and that once it has, it is only the beginning of your work with your future magical self, and just the tip of the iceberg in your initiatory development.

Contact is also known as gaining the Knowledge and Conversation of the Holy Guardian Angel, and once it has occurred (you will have no doubt of this when it does), you will receive all future magical instruction or guidance directly from your HGA (via the means of manifestation). You will also discover a ten-fold improvement in your magical practice, which is when the real fun begins. There is no end to your work with the HGA, and so the Core Practice of magick is a life-long endeavour.

EXERCISE 30

1. Devise a ritual to gain the Knowledge and Conversation of your Holy Guardian Angel, and invoke every day.

15. Abseiling

Or:

'The Integration Of Magical Experience'

The daily practice of magick is the slow, steady climb of a mountaineer. With each day you get a little higher, and maybe a new perspective is achieved. But at the end of each day you must climb back down again because your supplies are just too heavy to take with you. One day you may even climb so high that you don't recognize anything below you, even your camp—and this is maybe ecstatic or terrifying—but you will certainly be straight back down again as soon as you need a shit.

Coming Down

The process of initiation is gradual. There are no sudden great leaps or changes into a new mode of being at any of the levels of experience. As you must necessarily return to camp (your everyday habitual viewpoint, which allows you to eat, sleep and interact with fellow humans), it is imperative that experiences represented by the zenith of the climb are integrated into the everyday consensual conception of self, when you come back down again.

Special attention should be paid to any ideas you must necessarily form after non-consensual experiences; it must also be borne in mind that these ideas are nothing more than representations, or metaphors, for the experience itself.

As an example, maybe you have an experience you might later feel the need to refer to as 'being one with the Godhead'. This poses no danger to your sanity. However, should you then decide you must be able to walk through traffic, as you are clearly God made flesh, then you would have failed to integrate the experience in a useful or healthy way, with only a possible relocation to the loony bin to look forward to. Believing in any idea you might form about a non-consensual experience, such as a mystical trance, out of body experience or weird synchronicity is akin to the mountaineer who raves about the wonderful view, when he is actually inside his tent.

BIG BALLOON

Ego inflation is perhaps the most common result of bad integration. If you mix the fact you experience (on a daily basis) things that the majority of people do not yet understand, an historical attitude of elitism, and the feeling of power that magick elicits, you can see that it wouldn't take much to convince yourself you might just be the next Prophet of the

New Aeon[14], or that perhaps you are under surveillance by a secret organisation hell-bent on preventing you from saving the world.

If there is one thing to keep in mind when forming ideas about these experiences it is this: you are not the first, last or only person to have these experiences. Many have gone before, and many will come after, because these experiences are a fundamental aspect of the human condition.

Besides: apart from your weird friends, no one really cares.

CURDLED MILK

Now, any discussion of magick and mental health would not be complete without mentioning paranoia, which usually takes the form of a suspected magical attack.

If anyone ever tells you they're under magical attack, punch them in the face. You can always tell them Eldrid the Bastard Warlock made you do it.

You see, short of a demon harassing your unmentionables, how can you tell? How can you claim stubbing your toe was a synchronicity caused by the Black Lodge of the Hairy Pit, when no cause can be apparent?

The fact of the matter is, you *can* be magically attacked, but you might as well as ignore anything you think is the result of a curse, because you can never be sure.

---

14. How many more of those do we need? I do believe we are now in the Fifth PanDaimonAeon of Horus-Maat-Set with the Age of Aquarius on the horizon and the Eschatological Singularity just pulling over for a quick pee break.

If you think you are being attacked, or that some evil force is watching you with a view to ruining your life, you need to re-read the Big balloon section again.

TRUST ME, I'M NOT A DOCTOR

Magick doesn't only pose a danger to your sanity. Yes, there is megalomania, paranoia and obsession; but there can also be many positive changes to your mental health through practicing magick. It is a privilege of the magician to function as his or her own psychotherapist. After all, who is in a position to know your mind better than yourself?

When practiced well, magick can increase your happiness and understanding of the world, as well as providing a means of exploring and integrating difficult past experiences or issues. Life can become *easy* in a way you never thought possible, and you can even lose your fear of death.

THE PROPHETIC NARRATIVE AS GOOD INTEGRATION

If we consider the world from the viewpoint of the prophetic narrative, the risk of paranoia and egomania are greatly reduced (for an in-depth discussion of prophecy, please see the previous chapter). Without causality, life becomes an experience instead of a thought about that experience. As such, where can ludicrous ideas, such as events being the result of some spurious evil force (as evidence of magical attack or surveillance), take root?

If there is no difference between yourself and any other phenomenon, how can the ego take precedence?

It must be remembered that I am not positing an argument concerning the truth of reality; I am simply presenting the safest method of integration I have encountered. You neither need to agree or disagree, but it is possible, and advisable, for you to corroborate what I'm claiming by *experiencing* these things for yourself by performing the experiment of magick.

EXERCISE 31

1. Practice magick everyday until synchronicity becomes a permanent adaptation.

WINGS

Alongside the benefits outlined in chapter 14, the invocation of the future magical self leads to a very specific positive result for the magician.

Traditions that teach a concept of immanence, such as Sufism, present a view of justice as an act of *adjustment*. As all things are holy, or part of the non-dual level of experience, nothing is intrinsically 'bad' or 'evil'. Any discord in the self or community is necessarily a result of things being in the wrong place, or things trying to do what they are not fit for. Justice is an act of re-aligning those things to their correct orbit, rather than any idea of revenge or punishment.

This must necessarily become the viewpoint of the magician who has successfully invoked his or her future magical self. Unhappiness is the result of forcing something to go where it shouldn't (although I imagine some people would disagree). For instance, no matter how much I want to be a presenter on a topical garden programme, the fact that I look like a camel means it's never going to happen. Yet my encyclopedic knowledge of shrubbery, and my skill at draftsmanship, could make me the greatest plant illustrator the world has ever seen, if only I could see myself objectively. Just as a climber (I'm milking it), after they have reached a certain perspective, can look back down and see the route clearly, devoid of any frustration or hardship experienced whilst making the actual climb, the same is true of the magician. An experience of surrender to the future magical self allows a complete and honest view of the constituent parts of your being. It is possible to understand each of the elements that make up all that you have experienced and how they have necessarily 'led you' to this point.

It is only then that you *experience,* and so come to understand, your natural function as an inseparable and necessary part of the universe. Once you stop trying to use those parts of yourself for things they are not fit for, through the experience of a larger perspective, your constituent elements 'fall into place' (they will necessarily function in a perfect fashion) and you discover that you have the weight of the entire universe behind you as a result. If you allow yourself to do those things most suited to you (which is something that must be experienced, not guessed at), you move into a much easier and happier existence, as all of your elements are doing what they do best (which always comes easy) and you cannot help but be satisfied.

READING THE WORLD

Once you have the experience of seeing phenomena in terms of *adjustment*, or of things necessarily having their natural place, you adopt a wonderful view of the world. I mentioned earlier that synchronicity as a permanent adaptation, or prophecy, equates to an existence where every event *means* something. Coupled with the advent of the invocation of the Holy Guardian Angel every event comes to mean something *specifically* in terms of your life. This doesn't mean the habitual delusion of solipsism, but the acute awareness of how your existence fits in with the bigger picture. Reality becomes a feedback loop, and some have even sworn 'I will interpret every phenomenon as a particular dealing of God with my soul' in an effort to facilitate such a world view (see chapter 7 for my take on magical oaths).

SHINY HAPPY PEOPLE

Most of the time, we entertain ideas that are completely at odds with experience. We exalt certain ideas over others (such as 'TV presenter' over 'plant illustrator') usually as a result of cultural and environmental conditioning. We believe certain phenomena are 'wrong' or 'bad' because they are not the same as those things we decide are 'correct' or 'good'. This can spell a lifetime of misery if you happen to *be* one of your 'bad' ideas.

However, the perspective of the future magical self allows existence to be experienced as essentially perfect *by the very fact that it exists*, because value does not apply. Does this mean that a smack in the face doesn't hurt, or that Hitler was a swell guy?

No—this isn't a denial of actual experience, but its embrace. Pain and suffering hurt just as much as they always did, but they are allowed to arise and pass with indifferent acceptance. Can you imagine a world devoid of what might be considered bad? To do so, that world would necessarily have to be devoid of good. The Knowledge and Conversation of the Holy Guardian Angel is therefore a move beyond good and evil.

A genuine experience of a world saturated with meaning will engender a unique feeling of certitude. Knowing through experience that everything is in its 'right place', or that you are necessarily part of a process that is perfect, you cannot help but *understand* that everything is not only going to be alright, but absolutely fan-fucking-tastic in the long run.

How compatible is a fear of the future with such an understanding, when it has been gained through actual experience?

Lab Coat

As wonderful as everything in this chapter sounds, it is imperative you do not accept it at face value. The contents of the book are just one person's take on magick—how much of it is therefore likely to be inaccurate, misrepresented or just plain folly?

It's very tempting when it comes to magick, especially as a beginner, to talk a lot about the ideas presented in magical texts as if they were the truth; but if the experiment is not performed, and the results are not verified by independent enquiry, then any discussion or opinion of those ideas is essentially meaningless.

Remember: If you don't practice, you don't get to vote!

16. But Someone Would Have Told Me!

Or:

'The Definition Of Magick'

Hopefully, a definition of magick will reflect the magical experience of the person proffering it; otherwise, we're listening to a charlatan. As such, a definition can be as profound as 'magick is the science and art of causing change to occur in conformity with will[15]' (and thinking about that for a second implies a lot more than just a description of a magical ritual), or as downright shallow as a 'set of tools'.

The definition I offer is an attempt at accounting for all the various aspects of magick described in the previous chapters of this book, which are all informed by actual *experience* (and if you have been doing the exercises, hopefully you will find this definition satisfactory).

Here it is:

Magick is the art, science and culture of experiencing truth.

---

15. See Aleister Crowley's *Magick in Theory and Practice.*

This definition recognises that:

Magick is the art of experiencing truth. In other words, you can choose any experience (say, dancing around in your underpants), decide what that experience will mean ('it will rain'), undergo the experience (perform the dance), thus rendering the given meaning true (it will rain, because I have experienced the fact 'it will rain'. Experience is the truth). See chapter 3 for more on this. What can be experienced using magick is limited only by your imagination (the subjective), but how that experience manifests is limited by the available means of manifestation (the objective).

Magick is the science of experiencing truth. The truth isn't simply an idea, nor is it found in the relative or arbitrary nature of ideas; truth is experiential, and the practice of magick will lead you to an understanding of existence based on direct experience, not speculation. By its very nature, life is revelatory and so more incredible than any word or idea we can ascribe to it. You need only perform the experiment and corroborate this for yourself!

Magick is the culture of experiencing truth. Magick necessarily includes sociological and ethical implications, whether they are consciously addressed or not. These range from whatever magical tradition, aesthetic, teaching or approach you ascribe to, to how you tackle the endless ethical dilemmas you will face on an ongoing basis as a magician. See chapter 1 for more on this.

Magick is not simply a method of manifesting material results, nor is meditation simply mysticism. There is no distinction between Western and Eastern methods of experiencing the truth; there is, and always has been, only one movement, one school, and one aim; in the West, we know it as magick.

Simplicity

It is the simplicity of magick that prevents every man, woman and child on this planet from realising that they have the ability to fashion their reality as they see fit.

What follows below is not an attempt at providing an explanation for *why* or *how* magick works, but an illustration of the fact that *experience is the truth*:

If I decide that an experience means 'I will meet an alien', and I undergo that experience, I will have had an experience that means 'I will meet an alien'; that experience is true, and so as it is in a future tense, I must necessarily have the experience of meeting an alien in the future.

If I decide that an experience means 'I am happy', and I undergo that experience, that experience is true, and so I will have had the experience of being happy.

If I decide that an experience means 'I found some money', and I undergo that experience, that experience is true; and as it is in the past tense, I must necessarily have an experience that corroborates the occurrence of finding that money in the past.

Any intentional act is an act of magick, because an act is the rendering of an intention, belief or decision into an experience.

CLOSED FOR REFURBISHMENT

Magick means you can change as much or as little of yourself as you like. You can remake your history, take control of your immediate environment and dictate your own future. Remember: if you didn't make one of the decisions that make you up, some one else did. You must ask yourself: did whoever it was that made those decisions for me have my best interests at heart, or even know what they were doing?

More importantly: did they have any taste?

17. Row Your Boat

Humanity loves catastrophe. This is best expressed in the thousands of apocalypses we've survived. Again and again, from fundamentalist crack-pots to learned academics, we have been warned that the end is nigh and given precise dates and times for the destruction of the human race by earthquake, plague, famine, meteorite, aliens, God, cosmic rays, climate change *ad nauseum*. What can I say? We're pretty robust.

Yet our fervor for such delights isn't abating; on the contrary, it's reaching boiling point. To name but a few imminent catastrophes, we can expect doom any day now courtesy of Hopi, Mayan and Inca prophesies, sun spot escalation, the consequences of global warming, the peak oil crisis, and a Terminator-esque technological singularity.

I'm pretty sure that suffering, pain, misery and death features low on most people's 'things to do today' lists, so why this fascination with the extinction of the species?

GIBBERISH

Although the apocalypse is usually regarded as the end of the world (i.e. it will cease to exist), as depicted in *The Book of Revelation*, occult eschatology is concerned with not just the end of the world, but also the birth of a new one. In other words, the eschaton is the end of *a* world, not the end of *the* world.

The study of the various models used to delineate the numerous possible worlds, and their transition points, is known as Aeonics.

Imagine if you will, that existence is holographic—what is true of the part is true of the whole. Now consider the fact that we are initiates, going through a process epitomised by the future magical self. Would the same not also be true of the planet? Or the universe? Therefore can it be that not only is the world itself undergoing a process of initiation, but there is in fact *a future magical world*[16]?

Aeonics is for the world what magical developmental models or maps are for the individual. However, short of an advanced initiated alien race providing us with a developmental map of the process their world has been through, how can we know what to expect in the next step of our worldly evolution?

---

16. By this I don't mean a world where everyone is a practicing magician. What applies to the idea of a future magical self applies to a future magical world; it is a token representation of revelation, or initiatory development, but on a global scale.

There are three options: we make an educated guess, we use magick and make a prophecy, or we receive a teaching from a non-human intelligence.

An example of a model based on guesswork would be the psychohistory model outlined in *Liber Kaos* by Peter Carroll, and although no specific dates are given we are thought to be in the Pandemon (good, isn't it?).

The Hopi model, where 2013 marks the beginning of the Fifth World, of which there are seven, is an example of Aeonics based on prophecy.

Are We There Yet?

In 1904, Mr. Aleister Crowley, after receiving a little book known as *Liber AL vel Legis* from a non-human intelligence, was pretty convinced he had ended the old world (the Aeon of Osiris) and had ushered in the next, known as the Aeon of Horus. Although this immediately preceded a period in history so bloody and horrific we had never seen its like (which appears to have been prophesied within the text), a general confusion has reigned ever since as to the Aeon's actual manifestation. Did it actually begin in 1904? Has it ended yet, or are we still in it? How the hell can we tell?

Since Crowley, we have also had the advent of the Aeon of Ma'at (with another new book), the Aeon of Set (with yet another new book), and I do believe we are somewhere near (or in?) the Chaoist's Fifth Aeon (they don't need a book, apparently).

Which one is right? Are they all true? Why won't someone tell me what's going on here?

PEACE, MAN

During the 60s, the New Age movement hoped to usher in a new world known as the Age of Aquarius. Unlike magicians, New Agers know exactly what to expect. After the little nightmare we've known as history, the Age of Aquarius will be rather nice: there'll be free love for everyone, a species wide conversion to Buddhism, dolphins will communicate with us telepathically, and everyone will live happily ever after.

Thank the gods that hasn't happened yet.

I'M SO EXCITED

Based on a striking number of prophecies, the counter culture's current favourite date for the occurrence of the Eschaton, or the advent of the new world, is 21st December 2012.

On this date, the Fifth Great Cycle (of a 25,800 year precession of the equinoxes) of the Mayan Long Count Calendar will come to an end.

This date has been lent more credence as the end of the world by the work of counter-culture-mushroom-maniac Terence McKenna. Using the I Ching and a whole bunch of entheogens, Terence constructed a graph that demonstrates the influx of novelty into history, predicting an infinite occurrence of novelty on 21st December 2012.

What this predicted 'singularity at the end of time' will be no one knows, although there has been some New Age speculation that the entire human race will undergo a mass ascension to a higher realm of spirituality. Obviously.

And I Just Can't Hide It

In terms of humanity undergoing a mass ascension to a new level of spiritual awareness, you can expect, as a cause, alien contact, when our friends from space will teach us the error of our ways; some kind of cosmic ray or wave that will mutate our DNA, beamed from the center of the galaxy once planetary alignment with the galactic centre occurs; the switching of the sun's electromagnetic field at the peak of its sun spot activity, which will directly affect our pineal glands; the return of assorted messiah figures; or a forced reformation of society brought about by any number of natural catastrophes, such as floods, earthquakes, meteorites, etc, or nuclear devastation.

Personally, I hope they all happen at once.

Poo

Unfortunately, I do not expect them to.

Most end-time predictions are easy to dismiss if all they posit is some kind of catastrophic event. For example, hundreds of maniac astronomers claim a collision between the earth and a rogue astronomical body is imminent every year, and it's pretty easy to verify whether or not the evidence supports this. To claim that Jesus is going to re-appear next Thursday is unverifiable either way, so you might as well as forget about it.

However, what happens when you know for certain an event will occur that *means* the end of the world, and the birth of a new one, but there is no evidence for a cause of that implied meaning?

What meaning will the events on this planet have on 21st December 2012?

We don't have to look very far for an event, on that date, that might indicate a synchronicity.

BIG MOMMA

Mayan cosmology is intrinsically linked with as-tronomy. Our sun is known as First Father, and the Milky Way itself as Great Mother. The Great Moth-er is said to have given birth to the First Father in order to mate with him and create the world, with the black hole at the centre of the Milky Way as her womb.

On 21st December 2012, the ecliptic and the Milky Way will align perfectly with the sun. This is a specific, verifiable, astronomical event.

Mythologically speaking, the First Father will again have sex with the Great Mother, and a new world will be born.

Ooh.

Of course, deciding to see this astronomical event in mythological terms is only possible if we accept the astrological viewpoint. The Mayan prophecy of the birth of a new world is a divinat-ory result along the same lines as the Hopi prophecy of 'the end of The Great Purification' by 2013, or the pseudo-scientific synchronicities of McKenna's Timewave.

We're All Going To Die

The problem with understanding what all of these prophesies predict, in terms of specific events that will occur in 2012, is exactly the same problem found when attempting to ascertain 'where we are' in regards to Aeonics.

The symbols used within these prophecies, whether Mayan (astrological events) or pseudo-scientific (Timewave Zero), are a means of manifesting the results of divination. They are the equivalent of a tarot reading made for the world.

As such, a prophecy can only predict events or experiences within the confines of the meaning of the symbols used to make that prophecy. The Mayan prophecy predicts a new world will be born. It does not predict the human race being toasted by cosmic rays, an alien encounter or a nuclear catastrophe.

Similarly, the symbols used to demarcate the various worlds (such as the Thelemic Isis, Osiris, Horus model) are only indicators of what *meaning* various experiences in those specific worlds will have, not the specific events themselves.

Many believe the world is simply the planet earth, hence they see the materialisation of the end of the world as a global catastrophic event. However, if we consider the world in terms of experience, we can see that there is a lot more to existence than simply walking on a giant rock. There is subjective mental phenomena, such as attitude and disposition, identity and emotional experience; sociological phenomena from the family unit all the way up to international organisation; cultural experience such as art, politics, philosophy, religion, fashion, music, magick, science and technology; not to mention the various levels of experience outlined in chapter 9.

We can consider the world as the total possible means of manifestation.

If we want to know whether or not an Aeonic model fits our experience, we need to consider whether or not the symbolism used matches what is experienced in the various *possible means of manifestation*.

If we want to understand what a prophecy actually means, we need to consider *how the meaning of the symbolism used can manifest.*

The Mayan prophecy of 2012 predicts the birth of a new world: in other words, the occurrence of something new within the total possible means of manifestation, or a revolution in human experience.

The end of the world does not mean the end of the total possible means of manifestation, but the end of what currently manifests within those means.

Exercise 32

1. Investigate as many Aeonic models as possible, and work out how many different worlds we are in.

2. Investigate as many prophecies as possible, and work out how these prophecies might manifest.

Egg On My Face

The notion that there is a future magical world, or that existence is initiatory, is a result of realising that experience is revelatory. Any Aeonic model (and any personal developmental model for that matter) that accurately describes our current situation, and that which has gone before, must include the inescapable fact that existence is a movement towards truth.

For example, within the Mayan Aeonic model, we are approaching the end of the period in history known as the Fifth Sun, where the god Hunahpu has restored the kingdom of the First Father. In other words, the human race was prophesied to slowly return to an understanding of consciousness. The Fifth Sun will end and this understanding will be complete on 21st December 2012.

Similarly, the Thelemic Aeonic map puts us in the Aeon of Horus, where the Crowned and Conquering Child has come to restore the Kingdom of his father, Osiris. Again, symbolising the process of the human race gaining a new understanding of existence (the nature of which is found in the symbolism of Horus).

It's no surprise then that if we fail to recognise experience as truth, and existence as initiatory, any transition points within an accurate model must appear to predict the end of the world.

Humanity's apparent obsession with the apocalypse is a result of the inescapable experience of the initiatory process, without understanding what that process actually means.

No wonder there is a proliferation of nonsense concerning 2012.

EXERCISE 33

1. Using as many methods of divination as possible, prophesy the events of 21st December 2012.

EASY DOES IT

It is important to recognise that both the Thelemic and Mayan Aeonics (as well as many more besides) predict a gradual death and rebirth, from one world to the next. In terms of the Mayan prophecy, it does not predict the occurrence of a massive 'revelatory' event, such as a meeting with our space brothers. What will happen on 21st December 2012 is already happening now, but to a lesser extent.

So just what is this new viewpoint or way of understanding the world, slowly growing in our culture, which will eventually revolutionise humanity?

Exercise 34

1. Consider the following current events:

    At the time of writing, Iran is currently undergoing an explosion of interest in Sufism, with an estimated five million practitioners today, compared to just 100,000 in 1979; 73 percent of all American teenagers, and over half of British teens, are experimenting with the occult; and a team of leading scientists are actually conducting experiments, with mind bending results, into the nature of time and the phenomenon of telepathy, with the Global Consciousness Project.

    See how many current events you can find that share a nascent, transitional, or initiatory meaning.

2. Ask yourself: what does the fact I am reading this book mean?

RSVP

The revolution predicted by the various magical Aeonics and prophecies is intimated by the growing prevalence of magick (and other methods of experiencing truth) in society *right now*. The inescapable nature of experience as revelation is not just the basis for Aeonics, but its subject. All future states within Aeonics are characterised by a greater increase in the experience of truth. Revelation is always coming.

The understanding of magick is an increasing phenomenon within a growing number of possible means of manifestation. It is only a matter of time before it *is* the means of manifestation.

In other words, the future magical world is almost here.

RECOMMENDED READING

CHAOS MAGIC

Liber Null & Psychonaut by Peter Carroll
Liber Kaos by Peter Carroll
Condensed Chaos by Phil Hine
Chaotopia! by Dave Lee
S.S.O.T.B.M.E by Ramsey Dukes
Thundersqueak! by Ramsey Dukes

ALEISTER CROWLEY

Gems from the Equinox (if you buy one Crowley book buy this—it contains all of Crowley's practical instructions and holy books)
The Book of the Law
The Book of Thoth
777
Little Essays Toward Truth
Konx Om Pax
The Vision and the Voice
The Book of Lies

Magick Without Tears
Magick in Theory and Practice
Eight Lectures on Yoga

JULIUS EVOLA

The Hermetic Tradition
The Doctrine of Awakening
The Yoga of Power
An Introduction to Magic
Eros and the Mysteries of Love

GEORGE IVANOVICH GURDJIEFF

Gurdjieff Unveiled (read this first—makes many of his concepts clear and includes all of his practical instructions)
Beelzebub's Tales to his Grandson
Meetings with Remarkable Men
Life is Only Real Then, When 'I Am'

AUSTIN OSMAN SPARE

The Book of Pleasure
The Focus of Life
Zos Speaks
The Artist's Books: 1905–1927 by Dr. W. Wallace
Michaelangelo in a Teacup by Frank Letchford

ROBERT ANTON WILSON

Cosmic Trigger
Prometheus Rising

Illuminatus Trilogy
Quantum Psychology

Miscellaneous

Coming Home by Lex Hixon
The Invisibles by Grant Morrison
Book of Lies by Disinformation
Promethea by Alan Moore
Sex Magic, Tantra & Tarot by DuQuette and Hyatt
Enochian Vision Magick by Lon Milo DuQuette
Mastering the Core Teachings of the Buddha by Daniel Ingram

About The Author

Alan Chapman is a Western magician and writer, a Magus of the A∴A∴ and a member of numerous secret societies. His work has appeared in *Fortean Times* and *Chaos International*, and he regularly contributes to the award-winning occult website: www.thebaptistshead.co.uk.